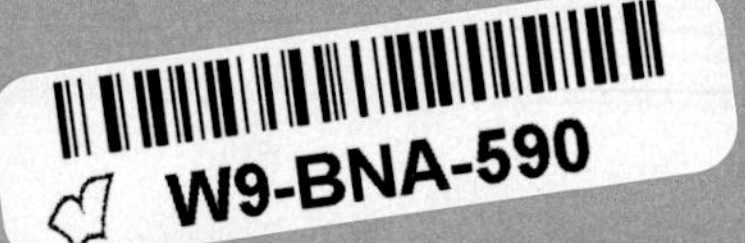
W9-BNA-590

BACKYARD BIRDS

BACKYARD BIRDS

AN ENTHUSIAST'S GUIDE TO FEEDING, HOUSING, AND FOSTERING WILD BIRDS

DR. JANANN V. JENNER

MetroBooks

MetroBooks
An Imprint of Friedman/Fairfax Publishing

Library of Congress Catalog-in-Publication Data
Jenner, Janann V.
Backyard birds: an enthusiast's guide to feeding, housing, and fostering wild birds / Janann V. Jenner.
p. cm.
"A Friedman Group book"– – T.p. verso
Includes index.
ISBN 1-56799-338-9 (hardcover)
1. Birds—Feeding and feeds. 2. Bird feeders. 3. Bird attracting. 4. Birdhouses. I. Title.
QL676.5.J45 1995
598' .07234—dc20 94-1820
CIP

Editors: Kelly Matthews and Hallie Einhorn
Art Director: Jeff Batzli
Designers: Patrick McCarthy and Beverly Bergman
Photography Editor: Emilya Naymark

Typeset by Classic Type, Inc.
Color separations by Sele & Color srl.
Printed in China by Leefung-Asco Printers Ltd.

For bulk purchases and special sales, please contact:
Friedman/Fairfax Publishers
Attention: Sales Department
15 West 26th Street
New York, NY 10010
212/685-6610 Fax 212/685-1307

Title page and chapter openers: © Carl R. Sams, II/Dembinsky Photo Associates
Contents page photograph: Medium Thistle Tube by Aspects; Photography by Jim Messina
p. 25 © Adam Jones/Dembinsky Photo Associates

DEDICATION

For my bird guru, Lanette S. K. McAndrews,
the Bird Woman of Mount Prospect,
who has forgotten more about backyard-bird feeding
than I will ever know.

Table of Contents

Introduction

"A book about feeding birds in your backyard should only have three chapters," my friend Glenn declared while we were floating in the local swimming hole. "Chapter One: Buy some birdseed. Chapter Two: Toss it on the ground. Chapter Three: Birds will eat it. The end."

If it were only that simple!

SO MANY CHOICES

Your first visit to the bird-feeding department of any well-stocked garden or birding store will demonstrate that bird feeding is much more complicated than Glenn's laid-back plan indicates. First of all, birdseed is a highly variable commodity. As you survey the different sorts of seeds and seed mixes that are available, you'll wonder what's best for the birds. Must you get pure Niger thistle seed or will the bargain bag of mixed seed do just as well for less than half the price?

© Richard Day

The ideal feeder should be sturdy, easy to fill, and able to hold several pounds of seed so you won't need to fill it every day. It should also allow desirable birds to feed without the intrusion of neighborhood squirrels.

To make matters worse, bird feeders come in a bewildering array of sizes, designs, and prices. There are feeders shaped like space stations, troll houses, ceramic mushrooms, and a range of architectural fantasies from barns and outhouses to lighthouses and miniature mansions complete with gingerbread trim. Even the variety of bird feeders that actually look like feeders can be confusing: the standard platform, hopper, and tube-with-perches designs. All this and I haven't even mentioned the slightly more exotic specialty feeders for dispensing nectar, fruit, and suet. It can be confusing. What should you buy?

NOT JUST FOR ECCENTRIC RETIREES ANYMORE

A quick scan of ads in outdoor and nature magazines will show that manufacturers recognize the potential bonanza in the bird-feeding market. Bird products abound. The incredible variety of products offered to backyard-bird enthusiasts is evidence that this hobby, once the province of retirees with lots of time to cram pinecones with peanut butter, has become big business. Once you become hooked on bird feeding you will have joined the 82.5 million people in North America who participate in this extremely popular interest. Incredibly, nearly one-half of the population in North America that is sixteen years of age or older feeds wild birds. And millions more can be found throughout the rest of the world.

MULTIPLE REWARDS OF BIRD FEEDING

The thrill of acquiring the perfect bird feeder or birdbath aside, actually feeding the birds is a highly satisfying pastime that can be as casual or as engrossing as you choose. Feeding brings the beauty of birds within easy range of binoculars (or even the naked eye

Nothing increases the popularity of your bird-feeding area like a reliable supply of clean drinking and bathing water. Birdbaths can be treacherous for some small birds, so make sure yours is safe and shallow as well as inviting.

if you feed them right on your windowsill) and allows a glimpse of wildlife that is otherwise unobtainable. The comings and goings at the feeder, the squabbles over birdseed, the arrival of fledglings, and the overnight appearance of exotic migrants all add a natural drama and extra dimension to our lives. It's also a wonderful way to enjoy nature even if you're not the rugged outdoorsy type. And bird feeding is a relatively inexpensive hobby, especially when compared with passions for collecting antique autos or carved Persian gemstones.

BIRD FOSTERING: MORE THAN JUST A HOBBY

Apart from these pleasures, what I call *bird fostering* (an umbrella term that refers to the general enrichment of local habitat for birds and includes bird feeding, bird gardening, and maintaining birdhouses) allows us to give something back to the environment as we bolster the well-being of the intensely alive, feathered nations who share our backyards and gardens. In one sense, we owe it to them. Not only do birds have to contend with well-fed but still-prowling house cats, but cities, suburbs, and urban sprawl also crowd the land that once belonged to the ancestors of our birds. Breeding habitats are fragmented and ancient migration routes have become tests of endurance across territory that is increasingly hostile to birds. Wetlands are being drained at an alarming rate, tropical rain forests are being turned into pulpwood and picture frames, and rivers and lakes are choked with pollutants. Birds are only so elastic in their adaptive abilities; when deprived of the proper breeding habitat, they inevitably decline. It is little wonder that as we learn more about bird numbers, many species show downward trends.

THE IMPORTANCE OF BIRD FOSTERING IN NORTH AMERICA

In North America, the situation is rather bleak. A study that was released by the United States National Academy of Sciences in June 1990 shows population declines in many of North America's songbirds. Of the fifty-six species of birds surveyed from 1978 to 1987, an alarming 70 percent suffered such declines. Many populations are dropping at a rate of 1 to 2 percent each year, and if this loss continues, songbirds will soon become rare on the continent of North America.

There are multiple causes for the declines in North American bird populations. Real estate development gobbles up and fragments breeding habitat, and deforestation in faraway tropical wintering ranges further dislocates birds. Species with strict habitat requirements return to the tropics to find smoking ruins where there had once been shady layers of rain forest. If habitat loss weren't bad enough, dangerous, residual pesticides such as DDT are often applied in tropical farmlands. DDT contributes to the decline of bird populations by causing eggshells to become too thin to support the weight of the parent bird who is incubating them.

In addition to becoming the victims of humankind's actions, small insect-eating birds are suffering losses from aggressive nest parasitism by two species of cowbird. Female cowbirds eject an egg from the nest of a smaller bird and replace it with one of their own. The parasitized species ends up rearing the demanding baby cowbird much to the detriment of its own young. Many species, especially warblers, are subject to such parasitism.

Even though the status of bird populations in North America seems bleak, the simple and pleasurable hobby of bird fostering may make a difference. Bird fostering is our chance to repair some of the damage human beings have inflicted upon birds and nature in general. Providing local populations of wild birds with food, water, and a sheltering environment, combined with developing a bird consciousness that supports conservation efforts worldwide, may be a force that is powerful enough to save our songbirds.

Although it is possible to build housing developments that enrich bird habitats, usually even the most pristine areas are developed with little or no thought to the wildlife that live there.

© Liz Ball/Photo/Nats

Creating a nurturing environment for birds can be both a helpful and enjoyable experience.

CHAPTER ONE

Water

Providing a constant supply of fresh water is a relatively simple way to attract a wide variety of birds to your yard. The bonus to the bird-watcher is that water will draw species who never visit feeders, especially insect eaters such as warblers and flycatchers, who hunt in the high canopy, and shy thrushes and vireos, who prefer densely shaded understory. There is even a report of screech owls visiting a birdbath. In the arid portions of the United States and Canada, a birdbath will be the center of attention once the birds discover it.

AVIAN WATERING HOLE

As they make their daily rounds, birds continually scout for safe and appropriate watering holes, and although it probably won't be instantaneous, they will capitalize on water when you offer it on a regular basis. Birds visit baths for many reasons, but thirst is their primary motivation. We generally associate birdbaths with lush, blooming gardens and mild weather, but this is a misconception because birds are thirsty year-round. They have three major sets of salivary glands and a variety of smaller ones to provide lubrication of the food they eat, but water is as important to their health as it is to ours. Because of the dry nature of their diet, seed and insect eaters tend to drink more water than fruit eaters do, but no matter what they eat, all birds need water.

THE BATH-FLIGHT CONNECTION

Bathing is a very important feature of feather maintenance. A thorough soaking, followed by vigorous preening, re-oiling, and a shake in a dust bath, cleans and realigns the microscopic zippers that compose each feather. Thus, bathing helps keep plumage in top-flight condition. The attention devoted to caring for feathers probably means the difference between life and death, because feathers not only make flight possible, but they also insulate the bird from extremes of heat and cold. Bathing allows birds to cool off on hot summer days and perhaps relieves the itch and irritation of mite and feather-louse infestations. Birds seem to bathe most in August and September, when they are molting, but many birds even take a dip in cold weather.

HOURS OF ENTERTAINMENT

Watch birds at a bath for even a short amount of time and you're sure to laugh at their hilarious antics and ridiculous postures. They vigorously splash, duck, shake, wriggle, and preen; some seem to enjoy themselves as much as children do playing in the sprinkler, while others seem furiously indignant at their mop of soggy, disarranged feathers. Once your birdbath is accepted by the birds, you will be able to observe different species' bath routines. And, if you provide a dust bath, you'll see a waterless version of the same set of postures.

Providing a supply of fresh, safe water will draw birds that would otherwise ignore your backyard.

© Gregory K. Scott

Your birdbath may be the only convenient and clean puddle of water for miles. Bathing antics such as these are your reward for maintaining your birdbath in pristine condition.

BATH ROUTINE

Once a bird has waded into the water, it typically squats down and fluffs its feathers. It flicks its wings in and out of the water, sending up fountains of spray. Then it wets its breast feathers and submerges even deeper, rocking its body back and forth to slosh water onto its back and douse its tail feathers. If you watch carefully, you will see it alternately transform into a feathered pincushion and then a scrawny, slicked-down bird as it repeatedly lifts and lowers all of its feathers. Presumably, this action allows water to penetrate to the skin as well as draws each feather through the water, removing oil and dirt. Rolling and submerging will be repeated, along with much wing pumping and neck dipping, until the bird is completely saturated and looks like an animated dishmop. It will then shake itself like a wet dog, sending droplets flying in all directions, and hop out of the water and onto a convenient perch to preen, oil, and rearrange its feathers.

HOW DEEP AND HOW HIGH?

If you watch birds as they bathe in the wild, you'll notice two things: First, they keep to shallow water, and second, their feathers get so wet that many can hardly fly after a luxurious soak. These observations tell you nearly everything you need to know about birdbaths; the watchwords are *shallow* and *safe*.

Because they drown easily, land birds avoid deep pools. Their cousins—penguins, loons, gulls, petrels, ducks, geese, swans, and others—have specially adapted feet to help them paddle efficiently. Their well-oiled feathers let them float like corks. Land birds, in contrast, have slender toes that are specialized for perching or hopping but are useless for swimming. Swifts, swallows, martins, and hummingbirds have the weakest, smallest feet of all. Consequently, they don't even enter the water, preferring to bathe on the wing or in spray from waterfalls (lawn sprinklers are a substitute that is readily accepted by hummingbirds). Woodpeckers have even stranger bathing habits. They never go to water holes, but instead perform all the postures of the bathing routine in wet leaves.

FEAR OF THE DEEP

Most land birds seem to have an instinctive fear of deep water and go into lakes and ponds only as far as the margins. They prefer shallow puddles of rainwater or places where creek or river water barely slides over stones. Your birdbath should mimic these natural conditions. There should be only two to three inches (5.2 to 7.7cm) of water in the bath, and the water should gradually slope to this maximum. Make sure that the birds have only a half inch (1.3cm) of water where they enter. In addition, if your bath has both deeper and shallower portions, both large and small birds will be able to use it. If you must use a container with steep sides, use large, flat stones to create the shallow stretches of water that backyard birds are most comfortable with.

ROUGHENED SURFACES

All birds will feel more secure if they can bathe and drink without losing their balance. In addition, they should be able to leap up to safety in a moment, without slipping. Make sure that your birdbath has a roughened surface for good traction. If you are using an improvised plastic or otherwise slippery tub, adhesive, anti-slip appliqués will give the birds good footing.

LOCATION

Safe is the watchword here. Waterlogged birds are poor flyers and easy marks for cats that lurk in shrubbery, waiting to snatch a mouthful of wet bird. The ideal birdbath will be free of shrubs for twenty-five feet (7.5m) and have low overhead branches for escape cover. The overhanging branches will serve two other functions: They will shade the water to keep it cooler at midday and will also screen bathers from the aerial predators who will soon learn that potential prey is splashing around in your birdbath.

© Richard Day

Suspending a birdbath helps eliminate places for predators to hide and stalk vulnerable, wet birds. If you try this alternative to a more traditional pedestal birdbath, choose a place that has some branches nearby to provide perches for waiting birds and shelter where freshly bathed birds can groom themselves in safety.

© Susan Day

A ground-level bath will be popular with many species. Here, a female house finch tests the water.

If your yard has no suitable shaded spot, the birdbath can be placed in the open, but this will limit its clientele to birds that feel safe in open, sunny areas. Shy, shade-loving birds will ignore a bath in an exposed location.

Finally, you will want to place your birdbath in a spot that is convenient for comfortable viewing as well as within reach of your garden hose. Perhaps the worst place to put a birdbath is near your bird feeders. Seeds, hulls, and droppings will foul the water in a short time, making an unsightly and unsanitary mess that birds will avoid.

PEDESTAL OR GROUND LEVEL?

Pedestal baths are not only more graceful, they are also safer if cats are a problem. Birds, however, seem to prefer bathing in a more natural situation: on the ground. You might combine the two by using a pedestal bath with a ground-level bath below it. This is especially effective if a drip bucket is suspended above the pedestal bath and if the overspill from the pedestal bath is set up to plink down into the ground-level bath.

One of the most convenient pedestals is a hollow plastic design. You unsnap the bottom and fill the pedestal with sand or dirt. A plastic pedestal has the advantage of being lightweight and easier to move about the garden. A plastic birdbath is much less expensive than a cement one, and it will not crack if the water in it freezes, which, unless you live in the tropics, is bound to happen sooner or later.

Do-it-yourselfers can make their own bird pools by digging a hollow in the ground. The size and shape will be dictated by individual taste, but the same rules apply: The finished pool should be no more than three inches (7.7cm) deep and should gradually grade to this maximum depth. The earth should be covered with black plastic sheeting, then wire netting should be molded over the sheeting to keep the cement pool from cracking. A homemade cement pool can be landscaped to look very natural and has the advantage of being able to accommodate whole flocks of bathers. It will require daily hosing to remove windblown debris, but the birds will love it.

Pedestal birdbaths also come in handsome ceramic saucers that can be either mounted on a pole or hung. Both look as though they would work well, but because they are so shallow, all it takes is a single, vigorous bather to empty one of these and the birder will have to spend the entire day tending the bath. In addition, most ceramic saucers that I've seen in use have been broken—either by ice or by accident. Their susceptibility to freeze breakage is a major drawback.

DRIPPING DEVICES

Try rigging up some sort of dripping device in your birdbath; the sound of moving water will act as a bird magnet. The simplest device is a pail with a tiny hole punched in its bottom so that a drop falls once or twice a second. Keep in mind, however, that the container should hold at least a day's supply of dripping water and that only a minute hole is necessary—not even the most devoted birder has the time to continually refill an empty drip-bath bucket throughout the day. A drip bottle, large coffee can, ample construction bucket, or similar container suspended several feet above the bath are all worth trying, although some experimentation will be necessary before your system works perfectly. A lid on the bucket will reduce evaporation, and a pulley will help you raise and lower the bucket with ease. You may also want to paint the bucket to hide it or even use hot glue to attach plastic fern fronds or silk leaves.

An alternate, inexpensive method to providing a drip is to use a garden hose, but unless you have a plethora of outdoor spigots, this will not be a practical solution to supplying that noisy drip to your birdbath. To make your drip bucket noisier, experiment with the range of sounds produced by a drop falling into canisters of various heights. A tall can should advertise your birdbath with a resounding and audible *plink,* which will be irresistible to the birds.

There are many stylish commercial drip fountains available; all of them seem to work well and all of them will help birds find your birdbath. They will save you time and may look much neater than the drip bucket you construct from the odd bits that are tucked into your garage or basement. Consult any issue of *Wild Bird* or *Audubon,* or see the sources listed at the end of this chapter. Because they run on electricity, most commercial drip fountains are best suited for patios or decks, where they can bring views of bird behavior just about onto your breakfast table.

The design of this drip bucket makes it pleasing to human eyes, while the plink of water into the birdbath below makes it attractive to avian ears.

© Richard Day

Although this backyard setup is far from elegant, it supplies an overhead drip that doesn't require frequent refilling.

KEEPING IT CLEAN

The only negative aspect of providing a birdbath is the grind of daily maintenance. Birds are notoriously messy, and windblown debris quickly accumulates in birdbaths and fouls the water. A dirty birdbath is a breeding ground for bacteria and algae, and both of these may pose health hazards to birds. In addition, birds shun dirty water. Once you begin to supply water to the birds, it becomes a daily obligation, but the fun of watching birds in their bath more than compensates for the drudgery involved.

The easiest way to fill and clean birdbaths is to use a strong jet of water from your garden hose. About once a month, you should scrub the bath with bleach or detergent to control algae and slime. A long-handled brush works quite well and can be tucked into your bird cart to make the job easier (see chapter 2, page 42). Make sure to rinse all traces of cleaning agent from the birdbath before you refill it.

© Christopher Bain

The simplest way to offer birds a spot for summertime bathing is to fill the lid of a metal garbage can with fresh water daily.

© Gay Bumgarner/Photo/Nats

A birdbath makes a lovely embellishment in any garden. Remember to keep the water only a few inches deep.

WHAT TYPE IS RECOMMENDED?

There is no perfect birdbath. Ceramic and terra-cotta are prettiest, but they'll shatter if they're dropped or knocked over, and a sudden freeze will crack them. Cement is strong and can support the weight of water, but cement is terribly heavy and it also cracks from freezing. Plastic is lightweight and won't be damaged by freezing, but if it isn't weighted down, it can be tossed about by the wind as well as by vigorous bathers. In addition, since we all want to reduce the amount of plastic in our lives, it's not very green to use plastic bird products, but sometimes there is no viable alternative. In freezing weather, only plastic works well because it endures extreme temperatures. Metal garbage-can lids turned upside down make great baths for summer, but cold metal is uncomfortable for human hands and doesn't work well in winter. Homemade poured-concrete ground pools are probably the best all-around birdbaths, but they are only practical if you have a large yard or garden.

WINTER BIRDBATHS

Birds probably need access to water more in winter than they do in summer, because local sources of water are often frozen for months at a time. Dehydration can be a major problem. To make matters worse, processed birdseed may have less moisture than wild foods do. When the landscape is frozen and snow-covered, birds will resort to eating snow to get the water they need, a habit that robs them of body heat. Birds who have access to fresh water don't have to waste body heat to melt ice or snow, which ultimately enhances their chances for survival.

There are several sorts of winter birdbaths, but all will be used mainly for drinking. In harsh winter weather, birds seem to know that it is potentially life threatening to bathe as often as they do in more temperate weather. The simplest winter birdbath is a shallow saucer of hot water that can be offered somewhere near your bird feeders but not close enough to become filled with seed and hulls. The disadvantage of a saucer of hot water is that it will quickly cool

Courtesy of Duncraft, Inc.

A clear plastic birdbath mounted on a high pole and set within viewing distance of your favorite easy chair can provide fascinating glimpses into the private bathing habits of your favorite backyard visitors. If you try a model like this and the birds avoid it, dry the bath and apply concentric rings of clear silicone cement to the inside to give the birds' feet something to grip while they bathe.

Courtesy of Allied Precision Industries; Photography by Tom Crawley

Birds need water, especially when most natural sources have frozen. The heated water you provide will increase the number and diversity of your backyard pensioners.

and eventually freeze, necessitating a series of trips to the feeder area to refill it. Immersion heaters are a more expensive solution to offering a constant supply of fresh water in cold weather, but make sure to use a heavy-duty outdoor extension cord and follow the manufacturer's directions to the letter so that no one receives a nasty jolt. There is also a solar birdbath on the market, which eliminates the need for electricity and its potential hazards. The solar bath is about as expensive as the immersion heaters, but well worth trying.

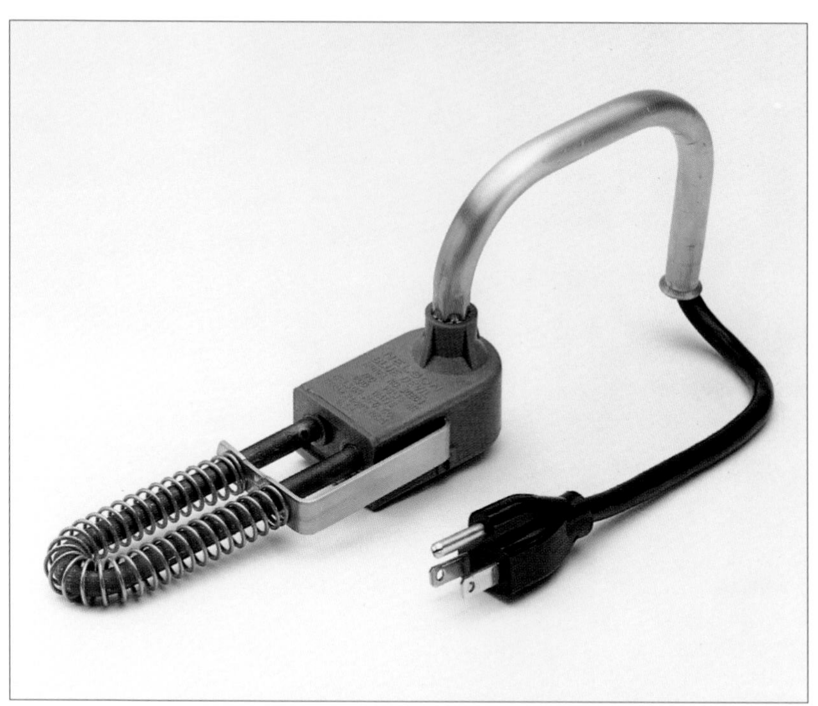

Courtesy of Nelson Manufacturing Co.

Don't let the looks of this immersion heater deter you. When properly connected to an outdoor extension cord, it is safe for birds, people, and pets.

The bargain-basement alternative to purchasing an expensive immersion or solar cold-weather birdbath is to use a heating unit that sets a light bulb below the saucer of the birdbath. The drawback to this method is that the bulb does not generate enough heat to keep the water from freezing at sub-zero temperatures. Winter baths will need daily attention, so placement that is convenient for the birder is crucial.

SOURCES OF SUPPLY FOR BIRDBATHS

CERAMIC BIRDBATHS

Opus Blue Bowl
OPUS
P.O. Box 525
Bellingham, MA 02019

TERRA-COTTA BIRDBATHS

Leaf Birdbath and Green-Glazed Birdbath, Hanging or Standing
GARDENER'S EDEN MAIL ORDER DEPARTMENT
P.O. Box 7307
San Francisco, CA 94120-7307
1-800-822-9600

Terra-Cotta Birdbath
SMITH & HAWKEN
25 Corte Madera
Mill Valley, CA 94941
(415) 383-2000

PLASTIC BIRDBATHS

Garden Scene Bath
DURACO PRODUCTS, INC.
Available in chain stores such as WalMart across the United States.

Universal Water Dish
OL' SAM PEABODY CO.
109 N. Main Street
P.O. Box 316
Berrien Springs, MI 49103
(616) 471-4031

IMMERSION HEATERS

Nelson Birdbath Heater ("Blue Devil" Model 30204, "Cedar Line Heated Birdbath," and Olio Birdbath Heater)
NELSON MFG. CPO.
3049 12th Street SW
P.O. Box 636, Dept. W.
Cedar Rapids, IA 52406
(319) 363-2607

Oasis Birdbath Heater
AUDUBON WORKSHOP
1-800-322-9464

SOLAR BIRDBATHS

Solar Sipper ("Model STDSS Solar Black")
HAPPY BIRD CORP.
479 South Street
Foxboro, MA 02035

DRIP BATHS

"The Deck Oasis" with "Oasis Dripper" or the "Stand-by Oasis"
AUDUBON WORKSHOP
1-800-322-9464

"The Dripper"
OL' SAM PEABODY CO.
109 N. Main Street
P.O. Box 316
Berrien Springs, MI 49103
(616) 471-4031

© Richard Day

An immersion heater keeps the water in this roomy, concrete birdbath warm and allows it to be used in the winter, without worry that freezing water will crack it. This method is not advised if winter storms disrupt your electric service.

CHAPTER TWO

Planning Your Feeding Area

THINK LIKE A BIRD

You've got to think like a bird in order to plan a successful bird-feeding area. Most people do not realize that although the kind of food served in the feeder is important, the design and placement of your bird feeders will drastically alter the feathered clientele who frequent your yard. Although we tend to think of birds as free-flying spirits, they are actually quite rigid in their feeding habits. Backyard birds ordinarily include seed, fruit, and insect eaters as well as nectar sippers, but only a small number of species are omnivorous. Common crows, blue jays, and grackles are exceptional in the wide spectrum of foods they eat, but an Anna's hummingbird will starve to death surrounded by sunflower seeds. A kingbird scorns all food except insects, while grosbeaks prefer to eat large, tough seeds. Birds also specialize in feeding in different strata of vegetation, and this affects their behavior at bird feeders. For example, doves are ground feeders who never cling to hanging feeders; woodpeckers (except the northern flicker) hardly ever feed on the ground, but rather favor suspended vertical or horizontal suet feeders; many birds prefer to hunt for insects in the highest treetops and are never drawn to seed feeders; while the vast majority of seed eaters prefer their table to be set about five feet off the ground.

DECISIONS, DECISIONS

Because few homes are designed with bird feeding in mind, the initial planning of your feeder area may present problems. Most houses look inward; they are made to be seen rather than for seeing. You may find that your home doesn't have a perfect place for bird feeding and bird viewing, and like most people, you'll be forced to improvise. As you visualize your bird-feeding area, keep in mind that it must combine these features.

1. It should be visible from your favorite chair (or a comfortable substitute), because once the birds start arriving, you will want to sit and watch them.
2. It should be sufficiently private as birds have terrible table manners and you don't want their mess to detract from the appearance of your property.
3. It should be protected from cold winds.
4. It should offer cover where birds can escape from predators, but it should not be so close to bushes that it becomes a cat-feeding area.

© Kent & Donna Dannen

This mountain chickadee is feeding from a mugful of homemade bird treat. The coated wire provides a secure perch, and the small size of this feeder may spark ideas of how to devise a winter feeder that will bring birds right to your window.

© Deborah M. Crowell/Photo/Nats

© Kent and Donna Dannen

The branches added to this hopper feeder (above left) give birds such as this black-capped chickadee places to land, while the baffle keeps marauding cats and opportunistic squirrels away. The value of perches on a hopper feeder (above right) becomes obvious when viewed from this angle. Because of their strategic location, perches allow birds to feed while excluding their droppings and keeping the feeder clean. If you choose a wooden pole to support your feeder and don't add a baffle, however, you will soon be host to neighborhood cats, squirrels, and even raccoons.

5. It should be easily accessible for servicing of feeders in freezing weather.

Also remember that if you have snowy winters, you must plan how snowdrift, snowfall, and snow-shoveling patterns will alter the accessibility and safety of your feeder area.

TO POLE-MOUNT OR SUSPEND — THAT IS THE QUESTION

Backyard bird feeders are typically suspended from tree limbs or are mounted or suspended from free-standing poles or posts. Before you decide on any of these options, consider the squirrel populations in your neighborhood, and take into account that an average gray squirrel can leap spans of eight to nine feet (2.4 to 2.7m), can shinny up unprotected metal poles, can scamper across electrical lines, and can leap four to five feet (1.2 to 1.5m) off the ground to raid your birdseed. Squirrels are a force to be reckoned with. They scare off the birds you want to attract and monopolize your feeders; they will even gnaw and destroy most wooden and plastic feeders. (See chapter 7 for more information on squirrels.) Even if there are no squirrels in your backyard right now, rodent intelligence is ever vigilant, and the local bushy-tails will soon learn that your backyard has a store of yummy goodies. An unprotected feeder is a potential squirrel diner, so it is better to account for these furry creatures in your initial plan. Some experts are so wary of squirrels that they advise against hanging a feeder from any tree, favoring baffle-defended, freestanding metal poles exclusively.

POLES: METAL VERSUS WOOD

Let's face it: There is nothing pretty about the metal poles that are typical of backyard bird feeders. Though functional, they are hardly objects of aesthetic beauty. The advantage of metal poles over wooden posts is that metal does not rot and its slick surface makes attacks by cats, raccoons, opossums, and squirrels more difficult. Wooden posts can be made more attractive; they are also more expensive. Because of their more permanent nature, wooden posts are also a poor choice for the beginner, who will probably need to move a bird feeder several times before finding the perfect site. While most mammals can easily climb wooden posts, metal poles are a more difficult but not insurmountable challenge. A metal pole greased with petroleum jelly will provide you with some burlesque laughs as your backyard nemeses take a few pratfalls, but swipes of squirrel fur remove grease nicely, and this hilarious method of squirrel defense will be short-lived. You might try flavoring your anti-squirrel grease with cayenne pepper to further deter them, but this, too, will be only a temporary solution.

BAFFLES

Baffles, large cones constructed of an ungnawable metal and mounted below a feeder, provide the best defense. If you can't find any commercially made metal baffles in your area (and if you don't have a specialty birding or garden store in your area, metal baffles will be difficult to locate), anyone who is handy with tools can make a large and effective baffle by following the instructions on the next page. The size of your baffle will be governed by the size of your pole and feeder, but it is better to have a larger, rather than a smaller, metal baffle below your feeder. So that squirrels don't just leap above the baffle, mount it four and a half feet (1.35m) above the ground. Be prepared to move it higher if your squirrels are exceptionally athletic.

Wooden posts can be defended with metal baffles, too, but the combination of metal baffle and metal pole looks nicer than most metal baffles I've seen on wooden posts. The latter seldom go together and always seem as mismatched as hiking boots worn with an evening gown. In addition, some metal poles come with multiple arms, allowing you to concentrate several feeders in one spot, making viewing and servicing easier.

This attractive baffle comes with its own hardware, which makes it easy to attach to a pole. The only potential problem with this baffle is its material: Because it is not made of Lexan, squirrels will be able to gnaw their way through it to feast at your feeder.

PLASTIC BAFFLES: CAVEATS

Plastic baffles, designed to swivel beneath the weight of a marauding squirrel and tip the animal down to the ground, have the advantages of being lightweight and attractive as well as easier to find than metal baffles. If they work, plastic baffles disappear into the landscape while they protect suspended feeders from squirrels and rain. Their disadvantage centers around the material that they're made of. Unless it's Lexan or another heavy-duty polycarbonate plastic, squirrels will gnaw through it to get to the birdseed beyond.

© Richard Day

This baffle will be effective—at least for a while, depending upon how intelligent and athletic your squirrels are—but try placing yours farther up the pole so that most squirrels won't be able to leap over it in a single bound.

MAIL-ORDER SOURCES OF BIRD POLES

Unless you are a do-it-yourselfer, finding a pole for mounting bird feeders may be a problem. There are several mail-order sources (for example, Heath Manufacturing Company, P.O. Box 105, Coopersville, MI 49404-1239, 1-800-678-8183 and Ol' Sam Peabody Co., 109 North Main Street, P.O. Box 316, Berrien Springs, MI 49103, 616-471-4031) that will send catalogs. In them, you will find less expensive triple-hanger poles and more elegant—and more expensive—wrought-iron poles with a pair of arms. If you want to hang more than three feeders, there are less expensive galvanized poles that come with ground sockets and mounting plates. Optional cross arms are available for these.

When buying a metal pole, perhaps the best solution is to buy one that comes with a ground socket. At your feeder site, dig a hole and sink the ground socket into a plug of concrete. When this has dried, slip the pole into the socket. If you decide to move your feeder, just remove the pole and put in a new socket at the new location. The unused socket can be filled with soil.

HOW TO MAKE A BAFFLE

overlap ↕ 1 inch (2.5 cm)

1½ to 2 feet (0.45 to 0.6m)

overlap ↕ 1 inch (2.5 cm)

hole cut to fit bird-feeder pole or post

tape to hold baffle in place

baffle mounted on bird-feeder pole

⅔ of a circle cut from lightweight aluminum

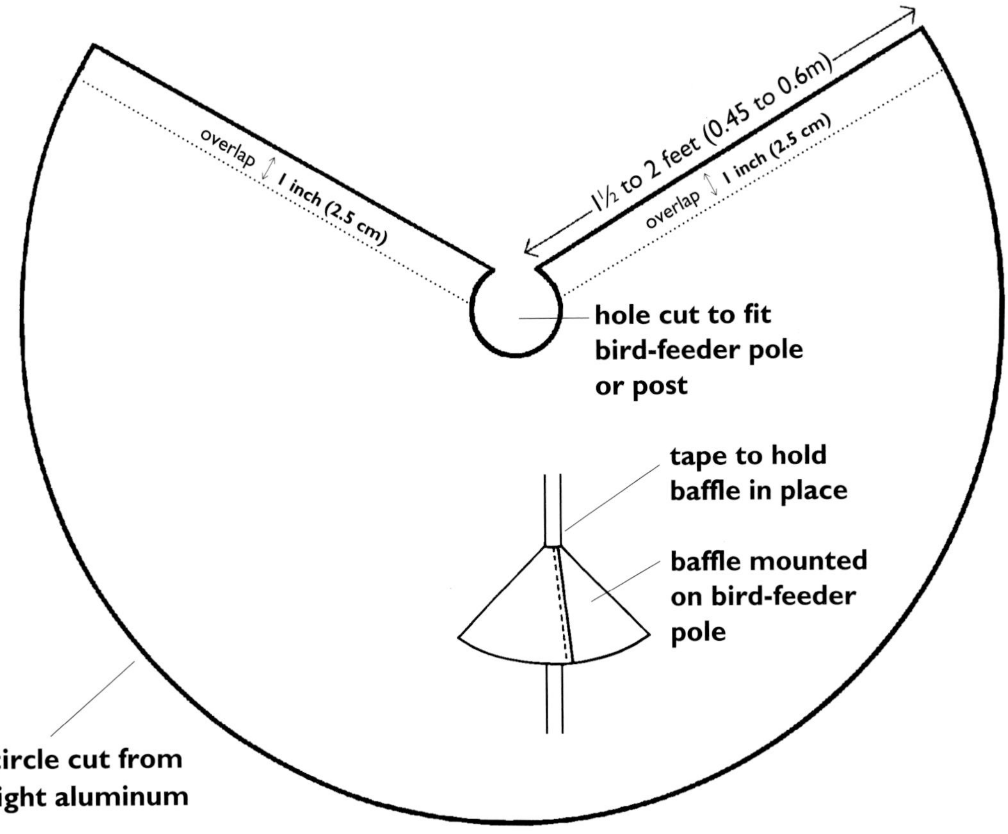

DOING IT YOURSELF: POLES

With a few tools, the intrepid do-it-yourselfer can make a perfectly serviceable metal pole from supplies purchased at most hardware stores. The pole should be long enough to allow the lowest feeder to be five feet (1.5m) off the ground. Depending upon the weight it must support, galvanized pipe measuring a half inch to one inch (1.2 to 2.5cm) in diameter is suitable. If you are planning multiple feeders concentrated in one spot, the larger diameter is preferable. The upper end of the pole can be threaded to fit into a socket that will be screwed onto the underside of one kind of feeder. With a little ingenuity, metal arms such as those used to suspend hanging plant baskets can be adapted to fit securely around this pole. Thus, it is possible to support five or more feeders from one securely mounted, one-inch (2.5cm) -diameter pole.

THE SEVEN BASIC FEEDERS

- A ground-level platform for ground-feeding species.
- A platform feeder to attract species that feed in low brush; some of these will be skittish about alighting on the ground-level platform.
- A hopper feeder placed five feet (1.5m) off the ground to draw seed eaters.
- A tubular feeder filled with sunflower seeds to act as a magnet for finches, a tubular feeder filled with safflower seeds to attract finches and cardinals, and a thistle feeder filled with Niger seed to attract goldfinches.
- A suet feeder to attract woodpeckers, nuthatches, and a variety of insect-eating birds. This can be suspended high or low as well as nailed to tree trunks for bark-gleaners, such as creepers and nuthatches.
- A nectar feeder to draw hummingbirds and (if you are lucky) orioles and tanagers.
- A fruit feeder to attract orioles and tanagers.

ONE IS NEVER ENOUGH

As you gain experience, you'll learn that one feeder is never enough, so don't be deterred from putting out your second feeder. A period of experimentation will follow, during which you, a willing pupil, will be tutored by your backyard birds in the art and science of offering the foods they want when, where, and how they want them.

It will quickly become apparent that you will need several different kinds of feeders to attract the widest variety of species.

GROUND FEEDERS

Ground or platform feeders filled with cracked corn and mixed seed will attract all sorts of seed eaters, including pigeons, doves, ducks, pheasant, quail, geese, a variety of sparrows, and some finches. The best ground feeder drains water easily and has a lip all around the edge to prevent seed from blowing away. Larger is better than smaller: Three feet by four feet (90 by 120cm) should be a minimal size. Scour your basement or the local dump for something to use as a ground feeder. My all-time favorites are discarded window or door screens, held a few inches off the ground by cement blocks and weighted down with rocks. The biggest problem with ground feeders is that the food gets wet (and soon moldy) whenever it rains. But if you keep them clean, the birds seem to love screens, and the uneaten, spoiled seed can be easily discarded before you scrub and hose down these ground feeders. Because they will catch seeds discarded by birds feeding above, ground feeders are especially effective when placed below suspended feeders. If you place them below suspended feeders, however, you are honor bound to see that they don't become fouled with bird feces.

PLATFORM FEEDERS

Also known as a bird table, the platform feeder is a raised, flat tray, with a lip all around. Many experts recommend this feeder design for beginners mainly because birds see food on a tray easily, and its visibility will lure them into your yard much more quickly than

© Richard Day

Bobwhite quail (above, at right) become quite tame and will visit your ground feeder, especially if you mimic their whistle. Blue jays (above, at left, and below) are beautiful additions to any feeder.

© Sam Fried/Photo/Nats

a hopper feeder filled with sunflower seeds. In addition, some birds prefer a platform feeder to any other. A platform feeder can be at any height but should be fairly large so that birds aren't crowded together. Two by three feet (60 by 90cm) is an excellent size to begin experimenting with. It can be a simple rectangle or any design that pleases the birder and can be made from any material sufficiently sturdy to hold up to wind and weather.

Like the ground feeder, the tray feeder should have a lip and many holes for drainage. You might want to use your tray feeder to experiment with offering foods other than birdseed. Orange halves that are speared so they stay in place, blocks of suet, chopped table scraps, baked goods, apple cores (seeds and all), raisins, dried nuts (including dried seeds from squash and melons), or just about anything that you want to share with the birds (including dried fruits and shot glasses full of orange juice) can go onto a platform feeder.

If you want to experiment with the individual preferences of the birds in your backyard with the intent of concocting a blended birdseed that will eliminate all the wasted mixed seed that the birds usually kick out of the feeder, a platform feeder is the place to do it. Some sort of compartmentalized tray is needed. I have found that a silverware tray, picked up at a local flea market, works well, but if you are handy with tools, you could make a compartmentalized tray from scraps of wood. Put a different kind of seed in

BLUEBIRD TREAT

- 1/2 cup oil (bacon drippings, rendered suet, lard, and recycled vegetable oil are all fine)
- 2 1/2 cups yellow cornmeal (not the expensive kind)
- 1 1/2 cups flour
- 2 tsp. baking powder
- 1 tsp. baking soda
- 3 1/2 cups milk or water
- 1/2 cup chopped nuts, dried raisins, peanut butter, chopped apple, or chopped carrots

Preheat the oven to 350°F (180°C). Grease your baking pans. Oblong or square pans work best, but pie pans can also be used. Combine the dry ingredients and mix thoroughly. Liquefy the shortening and add it to the mixture along with the milk or water. Stir in nuts (or one of the other ingredients) and pour the mixture into greased pans and bake for 40 to 50 minutes or until the bread is lightly browned. Put it into a mesh onion bag or suet holder to keep the larger birds from flying away with chunks of it. Extra can be stored in the refrigerator or frozen.

PEANUT BUTTER CONES

Peanut butter, bacon drippings, and birdseed are the basic ingredients in this concoction that attracts a wide variety of birds when it is smeared onto and into pinecones (children like to do this) and then offered at the bird table. Variations include rolling the filled pinecones in birdseed mixtures, using rendered suet instead of bacon drippings, and adding other treats to the mixture. Bread crumbs and crushed stale baked goods are two favorites. Graham crackers and dog biscuits ground in a blender will add extra nutrition.

SANDY DOGS

If you have a dog and cooking scraps (leftover pasta is perfect), your children may want to try this no-cook recipe.

- 1 cup crushed dog bones or dry kibble
- 1 cup sunflower seeds or wild-bird food
- 1 tbsp. sand
- 2 tbsp. peanut butter
- 1 1/2 cups rendered suet

Blend the dry ingredients with peanut butter and spoon into greased muffin tins. Pour 1 1/2 cups rendered suet over the blended mixture. Put the muffin pan into the freezer to set the individual "dogs." When they are firm, wrap each in a mesh bag (recycled onion or fruit bags are fine) and hang them all from tree branches.

© Richard Day

Adding suet feeders to your hopper feeder increases the variety of species you attract. Here, a red-bellied woodpecker and a downy woodpecker feast on suet. Red-bellied woodpeckers seem to have a broader diet than many of their strictly insectivorous relatives. In the southern United States, they feed on sunflower seeds.

each compartment and keep track of what the birds prefer to eat. This assumes that a variety of seeds are available in your area or that you are willing to order them by mail. (See sources listed at the end of chapter 3, beginning on page 52.)

The platform feeder is also the place to try Bluebird Treat (see recipe on page 32) or to offer many of the mixes of food that you can cook up for birds, if you have a mind to. Platform feeders are also an excellent way to introduce children to birds and bird feeding. Children can try feeding birds almost anything on a platform feeder, and it would be worthwhile for a child (or a school class) to keep a record of the food preferences of various species. The rules to remember, though, are the same for any table set for birds: The food should be fresh and clean, and the feeder should be checked daily and restocked regularly. While most mothers are too busy to cook for the birds, this is an excellent project for children (see recipes for Peanut Butter Cones and Sandy Dogs on page 32). It has the added bonus of teaching responsibility for living creatures and love and respect for nature.

HOPPER FEEDERS

In all its variations, the hopper feeder is the apparatus most people picture when you say *bird feeder*: a roofed box that is usually wooden, has two clear sides, and can be either pole-mounted or suspended. This model of bird feeder is the most popular, and there are many on the market. The advantage of a hopper feeder is that it keeps a quantity of fresh, clean, dry seed available. Birds peck at the seed that is accessible

FEATURES OF A HIGH-QUALITY HOPPER FEEDER

- It should be large enough to hold several pounds of seed.
- The material should be cedar or cypress, not pine.
- The top should move out of the way for easy filling.
- The roof should be leak-proof.
- It should be held together with brass screws, not with staples.
- The clear panels should be plastic, not glass.
- Look for a narrow gap for the seed to fall from the hopper out onto the platform below. If this gap is more than a half inch (1.3cm) from the hopper floor, small birds may be tempted to squeeze into the hopper where they will panic and eventually die.
- It must have drainage holes.
- It should have a small perching area or attached perches so that birds cannot defecate into the seed.

This well-designed hopper feeder has a mammal excluder attached to the pole. This excluder will keep rodents at bay: As a mammal climbs up the pole, it enters the excluder, runs into a dead end, and has to retrace its steps.

through a narrow gap, and gravity keeps delivering seed until the feeder is empty. The major problems with wooden hopper feeders stem from dangers from bacterial contamination that are associated with them. Face it: There are probably only a handful of conscientious, superclean birders in the entire world who *regularly* scrub out their wooden feeders with bleach to disinfect them. Most of us are unaware or too busy, or we ignore the problem; at best, most of us give our feeders a once-a-season cleaning. The perfect solution would be a wooden feeder with a low-maintenance plastic flooring, but thus far, I have never seen such a product on the market. Until such a design is manufactured, however, you can make your wooden feeder safer for the birds by disinfecting it on a regular basis and altering its design so that birds must perch to feed at the hopper. If this is impossible, it is worth experimenting with polyurethane plastic coatings that will keep fecal bacteria from multiplying in the crevices and corners of wooden floors.

TUBULAR FEEDERS

Hanging tube feeders are made of plastic and have portals that dispense a gravity-fed flow of seed. Because birds cling to perches and peck seed from within the tube, fresh seed does not become contaminated with bird feces. Thus, while tubular feeders lack the charm of wooden feeders, they do eliminate the disease-spreading potential of wooden hopper and platform feeders. The clear plastic tube makes seed highly visible to birds, attracting them to your yard.

© Valorie Hodgson/Photo/Nats

FEATURES OF A HIGH-QUALITY TUBULAR FEEDER

- It should have seed baffles and metal portals that are less than one inch (2.5cm) in diameter to help control the flow of seed.

- It should be constructed of Lexan or polycarbonate plastic, so it will not crack, succumb to squirrel teeth, break, or turn cloudy.

- There should be drainage holes in the bottom of the tube as well as in the bottom seed tray (if one is present) help keep the seed dry.

- The hanger should be attached not only to the cap but also to the tube to keep it secure.

- Look for a rain-proof metal cap that will slide up and out of the way to make refilling easy.

- Many tube feeders come with some sort of squirrel-proofing, often a metal mesh sleeve that is impervious to those ever-growing incisors.

Seed tube feeder courtesy of Aspects Inc.; Photo by Jim Messina

Hoppers and tubular feeders work by using gravity. By pecking at the opening of a feeder (top), birds remove seeds, and gravity pulls down others to replace them until the hopper is empty. Northern cardinals and a house finch (above) enjoy the rewards of a well-designed tubular feeder full of plump sunflower seeds.

© S.C. Fried/Photo/Nats

A suet feeder provides birds with nutritious fats that are especially necessary on cold days. This feeder offers a commercial suet and seed block to a downy woodpecker.

SUET FEEDERS

Suet feeders are one surefire way to get insect-eating birds into view. Woodpeckers, titmice, chickadees, nuthatches, mockingbirds, and starlings all love this source of animal fat. You can use something as simple as the netting from a bag of onions for your suet feeder or purchase a wire cage to suspend or nail horizontally or vertically to a tree trunk or limb. Suet is always offered in some kind of cage or bag for two reasons. First, you will want to keep large birds from carrying the precious morsel away to feed on elsewhere—usually up and out of sight. Second, you want to deter large birds, such as starlings and crows, from monopolizing the suet. A wire cage doesn't allow them to get more than a tiny bit at a time, while allowing smaller birds to eat relatively larger portions.

The suet you offer can be store-bought cakes or cakes that you prepare at home. In cold weather, you do not need to render the suet, but in the summer, when many people avoid feeding suet because it melts above room temperature and turns rancid, you should use either suet cakes that are purchased rendered or render and harden the suet yourself.

COLD-WEATHER METHOD FOR PREPARING SUET

Ask your butcher or supermarket for kidney suet (not "stringy" suet). Cut the fat into small pieces, chop it fine in a food processor, or have the butcher send it through his meat grinder. Melt the ground suet in a double boiler over low heat. Pour the melted fat into molds (muffin pans work well), and allow to cool and thicken before adding any seeds, berries, or other treats. You can add peanut butter, vegetable shortening, cornmeal, breakfast cereal, cooked rice, cooked noodles, flour, dried fruits and berries, ground bakery goods, leftover crackers, cracked corn, seeds, or even dried, finely ground meat to make a suet cake that the birds will relish.

WARM-WEATHER METHOD FOR PREPARING SUET

When the temperature rises above 70°F (21°C), suet prepared by the cold-weather method melts quickly, gets matted on birds' feathers, and tends to turn rancid. In warm weather, you should grind, heat, and cool suet as described above and then remove the solidified fat and allow it to cool. Then reliquefy the solidified suet, pour it into molds, and allow it to cool before adding any special ingredients. The second reheating drives off extra water and allows the suet to be much harder and less likely to melt and turn rancid in warm weather.

© Richard Day

The butcher at your local supermarket will usually save suet for you, especially when you make it known that you are feeding it to the birds.

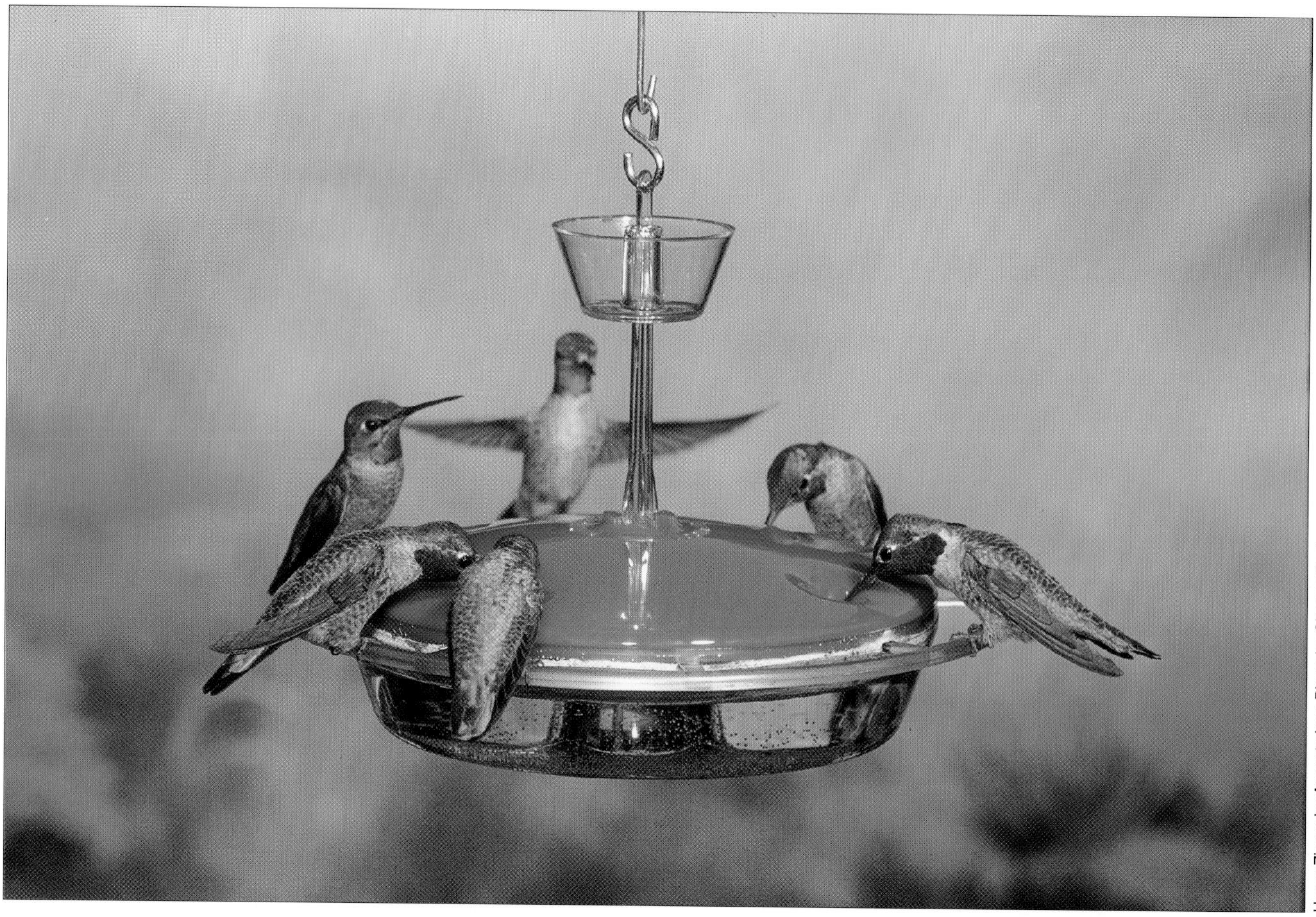

HummZinger by Aspects Inc.; Photo by Clayton Fogle

Hummingbirds (above and below) lap up nectar with their long, tubular tongues. Hang a nectar feeder outside your window for close-up viewing of these high-speed fliers, and you'll be rewarded with insights into their lives as well as glimpses of hummingbird anatomy and behavior that are missed when the nectar feeder is hung far away. Watch for their transparent tongues. Try to see their feet and eyelids.

© Tom Johns/Natural Image Photography

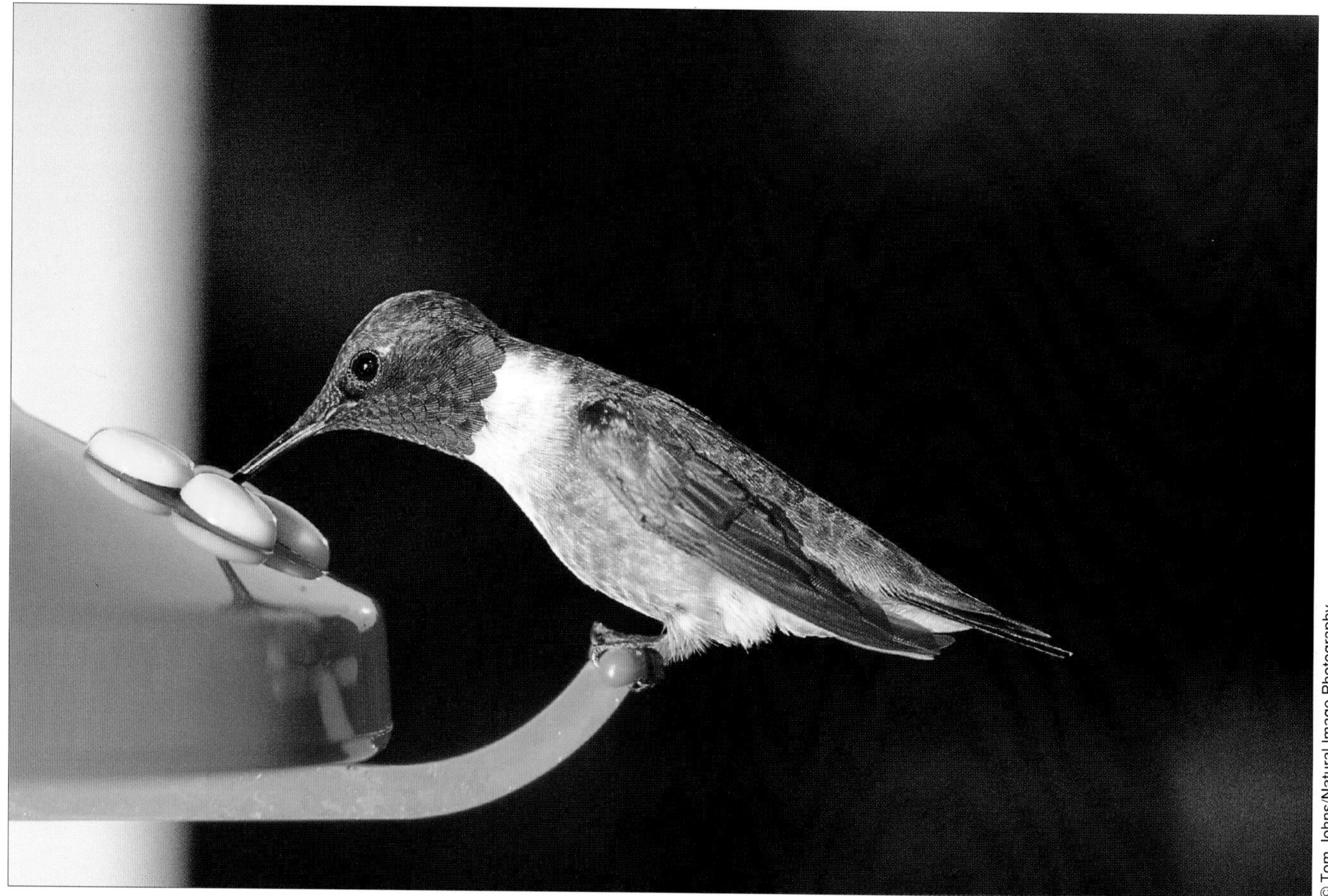

NECTAR FEEDERS

In the United States, especially in the South and West, sales of hummingbird feeders have skyrocketed. It seems that everyone loves these tiny, hyperactive birds, and feeding them is fast becoming a national obsession. Nectar feeders are inexpensive to buy and easy to fill and maintain. If hummingbirds are in your area, they will eventually find your feeders, claim them, and vigorously and vociferously defend them.

When you buy your first hummingbird feeder, you may be tempted to buy hummingbird nectar. Don't. Not only do you not need it, but it usually has red food coloring and other additives that the birds do not need and that may harm them. Hummingbird nectar appeals to busy folks who want to have a hummingbird feeder but don't want to make their own nectar. However, it couldn't be simpler. All you need is white sugar (not sugar substitute or honey) and water mixed one part sugar to four parts water. For example, mix one cup of sugar with four cups of water. Boil the

© C. Allan Morgan

Here, a female hooded oriole perches at a nectar feeder. Note the size of the nectar openings.

WHEN YOU SHOP FOR A HUMMINGBIRD FEEDER, CONSIDER THE FOLLOWING DESIGN CRITERIA

• The more ports the better, especially if you live in the West or in the Caribbean, where there are more species of hummingbirds. My favorite feeders have six plastic perches to allow the birds to rest as they feed. Hummingbirds don't need to perch to feed—after all, they are the best fliers in the world and experts at hovering—but I like watching them at rest as well as in flight. Feeders with perches let the birds slow down to human speed, if only for a moment. They are also best for introducing children to hummers.

• Before buying a feeder, open the box and examine the internal structure of the feeder, keeping this question in mind: Can you reach every part of the feeder with a toothbrush? Hummingbird feeders are prone to developing a slimy, black fungus on all internal surfaces. Every time you refill your feeder, you are honor bound to scrub its internal surfaces and remove this growth. The health of your hummingbirds literally depends upon your vigilance. What works beautifully for this task is an old toothbrush that's been bent in hot water until it has a forty-five-degree angle to the handle.

• Is the hanger secure?

• Is there a well around the hanger that you can fill with water to act as a moat to keep ants at bay?

• Because hummers are most attracted to red flowers, does the feeder capitalize upon that fact and feature red plastic on some part of the feeder?

• Look for a feeder with bee guards: small screens that keep insects at a distance from the nectar but allow hummingbirds' longer bills to reach the sweet stuff.

• To allow more than one hummer to use your feeder, look for plastic blossoms that are attached to the feeder. These will screen feeding hummingbirds from one another.

sugar water for about ten minutes to ensure that it doesn't ferment in your feeder. Allow the boiled sugar water to cool before pouring it into your newly scrubbed feeder. If you pour in boiling hot sugar water, a glass feeder will crack and a plastic one will be deformed.

FRUIT FEEDERS

Fruit feeders are only recently being marketed in the United States, mainly to attract orioles. If you are gadget mad or if you have a thoughtful gift-giving friend, you may end up with one of these plastic sleeves designed to hold half an orange securely. An alternative method to buying a fruit feeder is to spear orange slices—or halves of any fruit you'd like to try—on long nails driven up through the bottom of your platform feeder. If you don't have a platform feeder, spear fruit on leafless tree branches or tie it onto branches with string or monofilament. Once the birds have found your fruit offerings, you may want to make a fruit feeder by driving long nails through a piece of lumber and tying the fruit feeder (which will look like a miniature bed of nails) onto a horizontal tree limb (the dimensions of the lumber will be dictated by those of the tree limb).

Courtesy of Duncraft, Inc.

A nicely designed fruit feeder will attract orioles to your backyard.

© Richard Day

This bare-bones fruit feeder works just as well as—perhaps better than—the commercial types, needs little maintenance, and never has to be taken in for the winter.

SUPPLIES FOR MAINTAINING FEEDERS

Once you have set up your feeders, you will need to maintain them. The single biggest favor you can do for yourself is to be prepared for restocking the feeders and performing quick repairs. Having all the tools at hand makes it much easier to keep the feeders full and clean.

To start with, get yourself a bird cart, bird wagon, or, if you get lots of snow, a bird sled to wheel or pull your supplies to the feeders when they need servicing. My current favorite is a long-handled, low-slung, two-wheeled cart, but a little red wagon will do just as well. Because wheels don't work well in snowdrifts, consider modifying a sled or toboggan for this purpose. It would need only the attachment of a wooden or plastic crate to save you lots of time and effort in winter when it is absolutely necessary to keep those feeders full to the brim, which sometimes means refilling them twice a day.

The following list is a guide to stocking your bird cart with supplies that will be useful for taking care of bird feeders as well as birdbaths.

- Metal containers (rodent teeth bite right through plastic garbage cans) filled with seed. I have one container for sunflower seed, one for cracked corn, one for mixed seed, one for millet, and one for thistle (see chapter 3 for an explanation of the different kinds of seeds). These are periodically refilled from the large, covered metal garbage cans that hold my supplies of seed.

- A large-capacity funnel that makes refilling feeders easier.

- A stiff, long-handled brush for scrubbing down the ground and platform feeders as well as the birdbaths.

- A bottle of bleach (for disinfecting the birdbaths once a month).

- Sacks of grit and ground oyster shells.

- A spool of monofilament or whatever wire you use to hang your suspended feeders.

- A pair of pliers to fasten things securely.

- A screwdriver for making minor repairs.

- A pair of scissors (which always comes in handy).

- A step stool if necessary to reach your feeders.

- Suet and platform feeder treats added to the cart as needed.

© Richard Day

Supplies that are helpful to have on hand.

© Kent and Donna Dannen

Birds will appreciate careful feeder maintenance.

Male cardinals, chickadees, juncos, and fox sparrows forage in a mixed flock at a snow-covered feeder. The evergreen trees in the background provide shelter where these birds can safely roost and stay warm at night.

CHAPTER THREE

What Should I Feed the Birds?

You have now conquered two major obstacles in your quest to draw wild birds into your backyard: You have selected both a location and a feeder, and with any luck, your birdbath is in place and attracting birds to your yard. We must now turn to an infinitely more intricate subject: What do wild birds eat?

CONSULT THE LOCAL EXPERTS

There is one very easy way to find out what your wild birds will eat: Search out the wild-bird enthusiasts in your community. Every community, no matter how large or small, how urban or rural, contains a secretive cadre of enthusiasts who devote countless hours and dollars to feeding wild birds. The only problem is locating them. Some are as shy as brooding cardinals with a nestful of young, and many may prefer the company of their birds to that of humans, but everyone knows someone who feeds birds, and these are the resources you must cultivate. Consider their information carefully, however. While the advice of a local birder can save you a season of fruitless experimentation with foods that are scorned by the birds you want to attract, sometimes the experts are wrong.

BIRDSEED: THE MIX

Because most people buy their birdseed in bulk at large chain stores, supermarkets, or gardening centers, it follows that a commercial, mixed wild-bird seed is the most popular with people who feed wild birds. But is it most popular with wild birds? Most of us have little idea of the identity or nutritional value of the seeds in a typical bargain-bag mix, and because few seed companies have labels that tell you what sort of seed is inside the bag, I analyzed it to see what was being sold. If you have a supply of birdseed and a kitchen scale, you may want to spend a few hours sorting and weighing your mixed birdseed to get a better idea of what percentages of what seeds are being offered.

SUNFLOWER SEED

If you can identify any of the seeds in wild-bird seed, you will know this one. Sunflower seeds made up 10 percent of the grain in my wild-bird seed mix. There are two kinds: striped and black-oil seed. The striped seed comes in two varieties: black-striped and gray-striped. Both of these large striped seeds are used in candies and health-food treats like trail mix, and they're the seeds that produce the huge, ornamental sunflower plants. Black-oil seeds, on the other hand, are smaller, completely black-hulled, and are pressed to yield sunflower oil. While all three sorts of sunflower seeds are high in oils, fats, and proteins, the black-oil variety is richer and is preferred by the widest variety of birds. Titmice, chickadees, pine siskins, cardinals, evening grosbeaks, grackles, finches, and many sparrows prefer black-oil seed to both striped varieties. Because backyard feeding programs aim to foster excellent nutrition, a seed mix with a high percentage of black-oil sunflower seed will be

© Dave McMichael

Gray-striped sunflower seed is a moderately priced favorite of many seed eaters.

Black-oil sunflower seed is the most preferred bird-feeder seed, selected by the greatest percentage of feeder birds.

Its price prevents spray millet from being widely used in backyard bird feeders.

best for the birds. Of the 10 percent sunflower seed I found in my bargain-bag mix, only half was the black-oil variety. I am currently trying out feeders filled exclusively with black-oil sunflower seed and suggest that you try it as a first choice, reserving the striped varieties of sunflower seed as second. If you prefer to mix your own blend, add at least 50 percent black-oil and 20 percent striped sunflower seed.

CANARY SEED

This is the smallest seed in most mixes. It is a round seed with one slightly pointed end and has a glossy, yellow-white hull. While some birds will eat it, only mourning doves and song sparrows are really attracted to it. Nevertheless, it accounted for about 30 percent of the seed in my commercial mix. If I were blending my own backyard mix, I would avoid canary seed.

MILLET

If you separate canary seed from the other components and closely examine it, there will be a few seeds that look different from the others. Millet is a tiny, dull-looking yellow seed that has a conspicuous, dark speck on one side. It is a favorite food of many birds, including mourning doves, towhees, sparrows, juncos, cowbirds, and many ducks. There was so little millet in my sample of wild-bird mixed seed that I did not bother to weigh it, but my best guess is that only a small percentage was present, probably because millet is a fairly expensive grain, as compared with milo and canary seed. If you are concocting your own wild-bird food mix, include about 10 percent white millet.

MILO

This seed is also round, but it is twice the size of canary seed. It has a ruddy seed coat and is abundant in wild-bird seed mixes; it was the major ingredient in my commercial mix, accounting for 40 percent of my sample. Milo is the seed of sorghum, a crop that is grown for grain, syrup, fodder, and pasture food. Mourning doves and sparrows will eat it, although they prefer sunflower seeds and millet. I imagine that it is included in wild-bird seed because it is plentiful and cheap, but it is often discarded by wild birds.

BUCKWHEAT

This seed has a longitudinal split on one side, making it look like an elongated form of barley. It has a dull, light-brown seed coat and has little attractiveness to birds when compared with sunflower seed. It was also quite abundant in my wild-bird seed mix, accounting for 20 percent of my sample.

IS THE BARGAIN BAG A BARGAIN?

Everything is relative. Whether the inexpensive twenty-five-pound (11.25kg) bag of mostly undesirable seed is preferable to a twenty-five-pound bag of highly desirable black-oil sunflower seed at nearly twice the price depends upon the shopper's resources. Is it worth it to offer costly hulled sunflower seed (no hulls to leach grass-killing toxins into the soil—in fact, no mess at all), or should the birds husk their own seeds? Is white millet, an expensive seed, worth it? There is no doubt that inexpensive, mixed seed has a place in bird-feeding programs, but there are many species who will scorn your feeder if more attractive seeds are offered nearby. If the choice is between the bargain brand or no seed at all, however, the answer should be clear.

HOW SHOULD YOU FEED THE MIX?

Consider this scenario. Full of good intentions and overflowing with goodwill toward feathered creatures, our first-time bird feeder lugs a twenty-five-pound (11.25kg) bargain bag of mixed seed home from the local grocer, dutifully fills up the backyard hopper feeder, and settles back to watch. The birds arrive, but much to our bird feeder's dismay, some species reject the mixed seed, scattering it down onto the ground, where it becomes moldy or sprouts in the lawn. When the last sunflower seed is gone, the birds are, too. What should be done?

Apart from skirmishes with the ever-present squirrels, wasted seed is probably the most common problem faced by backyard-bird feeders. Some feathered guests (especially titmice) have picky appetites and kick out the varieties of seed that they don't like as they peck for their favorites. There are several strategies that will help you avoid this problem. You could open a cafeteria for the birds on a platform feeder (see chapter 2, page 30), offer them a wide variety of seeds, and let them show you which varieties of seed they prefer. If this seems like too much trouble, however (and for many people this will be impossible anyway, unless there is an exceptionally well-stocked feed and grain store nearby or you are willing to pay shipping costs), here are a few more suggestions.

- Use mixed seed and cracked corn in a ground or platform feeder.
- Use sunflower seeds (black-oil being the first choice, followed by the striped varieties) in a separate feeder.
- Offer thistle (see next section) in a third, specially designed feeder.
- Offer white millet in a fourth feeder.

OTHER ITEMS YOU WILL WANT TO TRY

PEANUTS AND NUTMEATS

If you have a ready supply of these on hand, chickadees, titmice, and jays will beat a path to your feeder. These usually don't make it to the bird feeder at my house—people eat them faster than birds do. Whole peanuts are taken by all species of jays and by titmice, chickadees, and white-throated sparrows. Peanut hearts, which are infinitely more expensive, are favored by starlings.

© Dave McMichael

Peanuts are favored by jays, chickadees, and many other backyard visitors who don't mind shelling them to get at the nutritious meat inside.

GRIT AND CALCIUM

As your biology teacher once told you, birds have no teeth in their beaks and thus depend upon grit and small stones lodged in their gizzards to grind their food and make nutrients available for digestion and absorption. Birds need and appreciate any form of grit you provide. Sand and old mortar (probably because they are good sources of minerals) are special favorites and should be part of your feeding program year-round.

The platform feeder is a good place to offer both grit and ground oyster shells, which provide a wonderful source of calcium; a shallow wooden box nailed in one corner will do nicely. If you cannot find a source of ground oyster shells (usually sold at feed stores), you might collect eggshells, microwave them or bake them for about twenty minutes to kill any bacteria that might harm the birds, and whirl them in your food processor or otherwise fragment them. Birds need extra calcium in the spring and summer, when females are using their own reserves to produce eggs and young, but it is a welcome mineral supplement year-round.

NIGER (THISTLE)

When offered in specially constructed feeders, Niger or thistle seed is a favorite food of mourning doves, goldfinches, pine siskins, common redpolls, and house finches. Because thistle seed is so tiny, it must be offered in a specially constructed feeder. It is the most expensive feeder seed, but a little goes a long way. Make sure to protect your thistle tube from rain. In many backyards, thistle goes moldy before attracting any goldfinches.

© Dave McMichael

Thistle seed is often called Niger seed because of its dark color. Members of the finch family such as goldfinches, purple finches, and house finches prefer it to most other feeder foods.

CRACKED CORN

There are two varieties of cracked corn: scratch feed and baby-chick feed. Some birds seem to prefer the latter, probably because it is more finely ground and easier to eat and digest. Try whirling cracked corn in your food processor to convert it to a finer grind.

Courtesy of Duncraft, Inc.

The reasons for the popularity of this feeder are clear: It has a wide baffle to foil furry competitors and predators, a seed tray to catch seeds rejected by feeders, ample perches and feed openings, and a secure rain cover to protect the seed. Most important to the birds, however, is that it contains plenty of high-quality seed.

Cracked corn will attract birds such as mourning doves, rock doves (pigeons), crows, starlings, juncos, grackles, house sparrows, ducks, and such fowl as quail, pheasants, and turkeys. Cracked corn is the least expensive of all wild-bird foods, so if you can't afford thistle, try grinding cracked corn finely and putting it into thistle feeders. Some people claim that the most desirable and colorful finches are attracted to it.

© Richard Day

Cracked corn is a favorite of many ground-feeding birds. Try grinding it finely and serving it in your thistle feeder.

BUYING SEED

Depending upon where you live, a birding store, Audubon Workshop, or grain store may be your best source of supply for seed. Although a list of mail-order sources for bird foods follows, it is usually much cheaper to buy birdseed in bulk at a local source. If you live in a rural area, feed and grain stores may offer the best prices, but these vary dramatically, and you may want to invest some time in comparison shopping before investing your money. Bird clubs, garden clubs, church groups, and PTAs often raise funds by selling a specific blend of seed that local experts have perfected. There is usually no waste in these blends.

OTHER SEEDS

- Safflower seed attracts cardinals, and it is worth offering in a separate feeder. If the birds ignore your safflower seed, mix it in equal proportions with sunflower seed and gradually reduce the proportion of sunflower seed. This may allow you to eliminate grackles and starlings from your hopper feeders.

- Flax, golden millet, sorghum, oats (whole and hulled), rice, rapeseed, and wheat have a low attractiveness to most birds, so it seems a waste of time to try them in your feeders. They are, however, ingredients of some bargain-bag wild-bird mixes.

© Hugh P. Smith, Jr.

The design of this spherical feeder keeps out birds that are too large to cling to one of the small openings. Although it does discourage squirrels, it may not be completely safe for small birds—they may squeeze into the holes and become trapped within the plastic.

INSIDE ORGANIZATION

Once your feeders are stocked, you can hurry inside to enjoy the action, and unless you have a window feeder, you will need binoculars to fully appreciate and identify your birds. I keep binoculars, field guides, a bird list, and a pen right next to the feeder-watching chair and enjoy keeping track of who eats what as well as when and how they eat it. I also keep a record of how often I refill each feeder and the cost and other details involved with the purchase of bird-feeding supplies. A year from now, I should have the data that will answer the following questions:

- What is the most common bird in my backyard?
- Which birds always move in small flocks? Which birds move in pairs? Which birds are loners?
- Which species are shy at feeders? Which are aggressive?
- What species make up the mixed-feeding flock associations for each season?
- What are the favorite foods of each species visiting my yard?
- How much birdseed do I use in a week? A month? A season? A year?
- How much does it cost to keep my birds well fed?
- What is the overall cost of feeding backyard birds?
- What does it cost per species?
- What does it cost per individual bird?
- How long does it take for the birds' curiosity to overcome their fear of unfamiliar objects? (With one birdbath, it took a week and a half for the first bather to arrive.)

Once you've arranged everything outside, the inside fun begins. Now you can put your feet up and watch the action at your feeder. When you first take up this enjoyable pastime, do yourself a favor: Borrow a pair of binoculars and spend an hour watching "your" birds. Unless your feeder is very close to your window (within three feet), the naked eye will miss a range of subtle colors and movements. Binoculars give you an intimate view of feeder events, and once you get used to them, you'll always want to use them to watch birds at your feeder.

WILD-BIRD SUPPLIES

The following list is by no means exhaustive; these are the merchants of wild-bird feeding supplies that I am familiar with. Most have a catalog that they will send so you can comparison shop by mail. The dollar amounts in parentheses indicate the cost of the catalogs; those without a dollar amount supply catalogs for free.

General Stores

CHICKADEE
1300-L Wirt
Houston, TX 77055
(713) 956-2670
($1.00, refundable)

DUNCRAFT
102 Fisherville Road
Concord, NH 03303
(603) 224-0200

HEATH MANUFACTURING COMPANY
P.O. Box 105
Coopersville, MI 49404-1239
1-800-678-8183

OLD ELM FEED & SUPPLIES
Box 57
Elm Grove, WI 53122
(414) 786-3304

OL' SAM PEABODY CO.
109 North Main Street
P.O. Box 316
Berrien Springs, MI 49103
(616) 471-4031

ONE GOOD TERN
1710 Fern Street
Alexandria, VA 22303
1-800-432-8376

WILD BIRD CENTER
101 Annapolis Street
Annapolis, MD 21401
(301) 280-0033

WILDBIRD COMPANY
617 Hungerford Drive
Rockville, MD 20850
(301) 279-0079

WILD BIRD SUPPLIES
Dept. WB
4815 Oak Street
Crystal Lake, IL 60012

YULE-HYDE ASSOCIATE LTD.
4 Lowry Drive
Brampton, Ontario L7A 1A3

Birdseed

BERKSHIRE FEED OUTLET
Box 317
Egremont, MA 01258
(413) 528-4967

BILL CHANDLER FARMS
RR 2 WB
Noble, IL 62868
1-800-752-BIRD

DAKOTA QUALITY BIRD FOOD
Box 3084
Fargo, ND 58108

GOLDEN BELT FEEDS
RR 1
Simcoe, Ontario N3Y 4J9

PRINCESS ANNE FARMERS' SERVICE
5651 Virginia Beach Boulevard
Dept WB
Norfolk, VA 23502
(804) 461-1580
($1.00, refundable)

WILD BIRD CENTER
101 Annapolis Street
Annapolis, MD 21401
(301) 280-0033

Bird Feeders

BIRD WATCHER HOUSES & FEEDERS
1866 Bell Road, WB
Nashville, TN 37217
(615) 366-6309

CARDINAL AMERICAN CORP.
4911 Grant Avenue
Cleveland, OH 44125
1-800-346-3425

SALT CREEK BIRDHOUSES
425 North Walnut
Dept. WB
Wood Dale, IL 60191
(312) 593-6791

VICTORY BUSINESS SERVICES
("The Aviarium" bird feeder)
9 Victory Lane
South Yarmouth, MA 02664
1-800-648-7254

NOTE: The staff at the Cornell Lab of Ornithology recently rated twenty-eight competing models of bird feeders. To obtain a free copy of this evaluation, send a self-addressed, stamped envelope to Crow's Nest Birding Shop, Cornell Lab of Ornithology, 159 Sapsucker Woods Road, Ithaca, NY 14850, or in Canada write to Long Point Bird Observatory, P.O. Box 160, Port Rowan, Ontario N0E 1M0. Ask for the Crow's Nest Catalog, too. It has many reference books and good prices on binoculars as well as bird-feeding supplies.

Birdhouses

ADIRONDACK ARTS AND CRAFTS
P.O. Box 1
Wilmington, NY 12997
(518) 946-7476

COOSA RUSTICS
Route 1, Box 560
Rockford, AL 35136
(206) 377-2362

INTERESTING INVENTIONS CORP.
705 Algonquin Road
Rt. 62
Lake in the Hills, IL 60102

KINSMAN COMPANY
Dept. A63
River Road
Point Pleasant, PA 18950
(215) 297-5613

THE WOODPECKER SHOP
Route 3, Box 187
Dover, OH 44622

Purple Martin Houses

CARROLL INDUSTRIES
P.O. Box 577
Dept. WB
Madison, MS 39130

MR. BIRDHOUSE
2307 W. Highway 2 West
Grand Rapids, MN 55744
(218) 326-2362

NATURE HOUSE
1-800-255-2692

Societies and Newsletters

CARDINAL AMERICAN CORPORATION
Advice for Bird Lovers
Cardinal Consumer Products Division
4911 Grant Avenue
Cleveland, OH 44125

DICK E. BIRD NEWS
P.O. Box 377
Acme, MI 49610

NATIONAL BIRD-FEEDING SOCIETY
1163 Shermer Road
Northbrook, IL 60062

NORTH AMERICAN BLUEBIRD SOCIETY
Box 6295
Silver Spring, MD 20916

PROJECT FEEDERWATCH
Cornell Laboratory of Ornithology
159 Sapsucker Woods Road
Ithaca, NY 14850

© Richard Day

Purple martin houses provide endless hours of entertainment as you watch the comings and goings at the openings to the "apartments." Be warned, however, that although martins dispose of enormous numbers of pesky flying insects for their human landlords, they are noisy, messy neighbors. Put the martin mansion far away from your own and everyone will be happy.

CHAPTER FOUR

City-Bird Feeding

Although my mother and sister have been bird-feeding enthusiasts for a long time, I resisted their efforts to convert me from bird-watcher to backyard-bird feeder for twenty years. To my mind, it was not nearly as pure as bird-watching, which requires a naturalist's specially honed skills as well as study, effort, sweat, and sometimes even blood, as you spend hours stalking tidal marshes and forest edges at dawn, hunting for those elusive warblers and baffling shorebirds. Besides, it seemed a moot point because I had no backyard; only four tiny rooms on the fourth floor of a New York City tenement that were crammed with too many books. And even if I could find a local source for birdseed, how could I possibly carry those big bags up four flights of stairs, and where would I store them anyway? It all seemed impossible, messy, and not for me.

Then I moved out of my New York City apartment and settled in the Alabama countryside. Now, not only do I have a backyard, but there is a front yard, side yards, and acres of woodland with birds everywhere. So with this optimal bird-feeding environment at my doorstep—and with this book in mind—I set about learning to feed backyard birds. Now I recognize that there is a difference between feeder birds and the wild birds you see after patient stalking and careful observation in the field. Those you lure to your feeders become your birds as no birds glimpsed through binoculars can. As you watch your feeder birds, you observe their individual behaviors and learn the idiosyncrasies of various species that you can see only at close range. Watch a chickadee flit into your feeder, select a single sunflower seed, and fly off to a perch. It will hold that seed between both feet and hammer at the hull with its bill. How does it manage to do this without falling off the branch? When the first seed is eaten, the

© Richard Day

Even a city dweller can enjoy bird feeding. A tiny sunflower feeder attached to a window will allow you to adopt a sparrow.

© Jerry Howard/Positive Images

Because birds who are well fed have a better chance of surviving cold spells than do those who are poorly nourished, the city-bird feeder may mean the difference between life and death.

© Tom and Bev Evans

A widely fanned tail showing a distinct border of white spots indicates that these ruby-throated hummingbirds are feeling possessive and aggressive about this nectar feeder.

© Steve & Dave Maslowski

This narrow tray offers a chickadee-size banquet.

chickadee will be off for another and another and yet another sunflower seed until you have grown tired of watching. Birds are natural entertainers who enliven the areas they grace—all for the price of a little birdseed and some water. Now I regret that I never fed the birds from my windows in Greenwich Village.

FOR THE CITY-BIRD FEEDER

Several problems face the city-bird feeder: where to put the feeder; where to get supplies; and how to get supplies with the least possible effort.

WHERE TO PUT THE FEEDER?

If you have no terrace, balcony, or even a postage stamp–size backyard, you should consider a window feeder. Here are several designs that will work.

1. A shelf with hoppers at either end will be secure and will not plummet to the pavement. The disadvantage of this design is that seed scattered on the shelf will attract doves and pigeons. Their noisy, rolling coos, the mess they create, and the breeding ground for aspergillosis their dung fosters will probably make this your least favorite design, especially if your apartment is small and the birds are intrusive. You can eliminate the disease potential if you scrub down the shelf regularly, sloshing a bucket of hot, soapy water onto it, and then make sure it is rinsed thoroughly.

2. Attach a bracket to your window frame and securely hang a tubular feeder to discourage pigeons and doves but attract sparrows, chickadees, nuthatches, and finches. If you offer a premium feed such

as black-oil sunflower seed or hulled sunflower seed, there will be little mess to attract pigeons and no problem with wasted seed, while the bracket will keep your feeder from braining an innocent pedestrian.

3. An in-house window feeder, actually a variation of a terrarium that brings the birds right into your home, is the Rolex of shelf feeders. These have one-way glass, and the best have a wide wooden top that lifts to allow easy filling and cleaning. But these will not work for every city-bird feeder. You must have double-glassed frames that are twenty-four to twenty-seven inches (61 to 67cm) wide, as well as a good deal of money to purchase this feeder. If you are a do-it-yourselfer, you may be able to adapt the design of in-house bird feeders to your smaller windows by fitting panes of one-way glass into frames that will form the side panels and viewing screen of the finished feeder. The side panels attach to a wooden floor, and a hinged wooden lid that lifts will provide easy access to the feeder platform.

4. The most conservative window feeder design and perhaps the one for a first-time bird feeder to try is a simple plastic feeder that attaches to the window with suction cups. There are several advantages to attaching your feeder to glass. Squirrels cannot reach it, and if it has a curved rain shield, pigeons will not be attracted to it or to the windowsill below, especially if you feed hulled sunflower seed that has little wastage. When shopping for plastic, suction-cup attached feeders, keep these questions in mind.

- How easy is it to fill the feeder? If you have to climb about and do impossible contortions high above a metropolitan street when the feeder is empty, your enthusiasm for bird feeding may be dampened. The best small plastic window feeders lift out of their moorings to be filled within the house and replaced back outside the window.

- Is there a rain shield? Have provisions been made for drainage?

- What is the capacity of the feeder? Find one that holds at least two cups or more of seed.

- Can the birds see you? Mirrored film on the rear of the feeder will hide you from the birds and let you enjoy them at close range.

- How safe is the feeder for pedestrians on the street below? If you live on a busy street, it may not be wise (and may be illegal and irresponsible) to use a window-mounted bird feeder, because eventually, the suction cups will fail and your little plastic feeder will become a potentially deadly falling object. But don't let this deter you from trying a window feeder. You might glue the suction cups to a board that will be attached to the frame of your window or look for a feeder that will attach to your window frame with a clamp instead of suction cups.

SOURCES OF SEED SUPPLY

Because storage space is usually limited or nonexistent in apartments, the city-bird feeder will not be able to keep large stocks of birdseed on hand. One viable alternative is to order premium seed by mail and have it delivered to your door at regular intervals. For armchair comparison shopping, consult the list of seed suppliers in the previous chapter and send away for their catalogs.

SOURCES OF IN-HOUSE WINDOW FEEDERS

Viewmaster
THE BROWN COMPANY
140 Dean Knauss Drive
Narragansett, RI 02882
1-800-556-7670
($2.00, refundable on order)

Meta Magic Window
WILD BIRD CENTERS OF AMERICA, INC.
101 Annapolis Street
Annapolis, MD 21401
(301) 280-0033

U-View Bird Feeder
CEDAR WORKS
P.O. Box 266
Moorhead, IA 51558
(712) 886-5425

CHAPTER FIVE

Bird Gardening

One of the most effective means of attracting birds to your backyard is to use plantings to create a habitat that offers nutritious, natural food year-round as well as a suitable habitat for nesting and cover to escape predators. In essence, you want birds to be comfortable in your backyard, and the richer the foods you offer and the denser the cover, the more comfortable the birds will be and the more you will have. Setting up bird feeders and providing free lunch and water will draw birds to your backyard, but thoughtful plantings will invite nesting residents who will bring their fledglings to your feeder. Your plantings will also attract insect-eating birds who never visit feeders, and it follows that the greater the variety of trees, shrubs, vines, and wildflowers you plant, the greater the variety of birds that will be attracted to your yard. Here are some planting suggestions.

Cover. Between 8 and 15 percent of the trees and shrubs in your yard should be needle-leaved evergreens to offer birds shelter in cold, wind, and rain as well as sanctuary from prowling cats and diving raptors. If your trees and shrubs include equal proportions of broad- and needle-leaved evergreens and deciduous species, you will attract the widest variety of birds.

Magnets. Some tree and shrub species are magnets for wild birds, attracting insect- and fruit-eating birds

Evergreens provide cover, foraging and nesting territory, and food for many species of birds.

© Philip Beaurline/Photo/Nats

Beeches are not only magnificent throughout the seasons, but they also act as magnets for many species of birds. Their masts provide food for many species who aren't attracted to bird feeders, and their spreading branches offer cover and nesting sites.

who will not be drawn to usual feeder foods. Magnet trees include (in order from most to least attractive) mulberry, tupelo, hackberry, crab apple, oak, sassafras, sweet gum, beech, pine, walnut, elm, birch, maple, hawthorn, alder, ash, and hemlock. Magnet shrubs and small trees include cherry, sumac, serviceberry, holly, elaeagnus, dogwood, buckthorn, and juniper. Low shrubs and vines that are magnets include elderberry, blackberry, raspberry, blueberry, Virginia creeper, grape, bayberry, honeysuckle, viburnum, spicebush, bittersweet, rose, and barberry.

Bugs. If you can increase the attractiveness of your garden for bumblebees, butterflies, and a wide variety of beetles and beneficial flies, it will automatically be interesting to insect-eating birds. To increase the insects in your garden, one of the most important first steps is to create a pesticide-free zone. If you use artificial chemical poisons that will kill many harmless and beneficial insects as well as the few that you want to eliminate, stop using them. Use companion planting to help control pest insects: California poppy and French marigold among the vegetables will draw hoverflies, whose larvae will attack greenflies. Aid ladybugs (ladybird beetles) by providing hollow plant stems for winter hibernation sites. If your climate is mild enough, insects will be present year-round in your garden if they have food supplies, particularly nectar and pollen. A shopping tip to keep in mind when selecting plants at a nursery is to buy those that are buzzing with bees, because individuals of a species vary in nectar and pollen productivity. In winter, nectar and pollen are at a premium: If your climate permits, try winter-flowering heather, *Erica camea*, *Crocus chrysanthus*, and grape hyacinth. In spring, honesty, broad bean, hyssop, and valerian are recommended, while in summer, yarrow, *Buddleia davidii*, and goldenrod are outstanding pollen and nectar producers. Michaelmas daisy and English ivy are good choices for autumn.

© Jean Baxter/Photo/Nats

In spring, honesty's abundant pollen and nectar attract a plethora of insects, which in turn draw birds into your garden.

© Cathy Wilkinson Barash/Photo/Nats

© Hugh P. Smith, Jr.

Hyssop (top) will draw bugs and birds, while large trees, such as a mimosa (above), provide foraging, feeding, and nesting territory for insectivorous birds and species that are too shy to come to bird tables.

Arrangement. It does little good to put magnet trees and shrubs—those that are irresistible to birds—in the back of your yard, where you cannot see them. Put them close to the house or deck or other convenient observation points.

Surroundings. Consider your garden as a bird might view it: as a piece of a larger landscape. For example, a bird might see the open lawns with scattered, small saplings as a short-grass prairie or as plains. If you plant a thick wall of quick-growing shrubs or a tangle of vines, the birds may see your yard as an islandlike grove amid the grassland. In contrast, if the surrounding neighborhood is heavily wooded, your open lawn may be seen as a meadow. You might want to plant shrubs and flowers that will enhance this effect.

Edges. Birds like edges or transitions between habitats, and you should exploit edges to draw birds into your garden. Make sure your tree-shaded, thick plantings of understory shrubs and vines are visible from the house. If your yard has many dense beds of shrubs, consider uprooting some and replacing them with grass and beds of flowers to increase edges.

© John Glover

This small yard is packed with microhabitats that include water, flowering plants to attract insects, and cover for nesting and hiding from predators.

© Carl Freeman/Dembinsky Photo Associates

Flowering trees, such as this apple tree, provide a beautiful, versatile backdrop for your backyard birds.

© Derek Fell

Fruits are irresistible to humans and birds alike.

© Richard Day

American robins (top) love fruit. They will linger in the northern states long into the colder months if there is a rich supply of berries available. In the South, robins form large flocks that will feast for days on berries of dogwoods and holly. An American goldfinch (above) finds an appealing perch on a branch of berries.

Messy. Don't be too meticulous in your garden. Birds seem to like a messy garden better than a painstakingly manicured one. Leave dead trees and stumps wherever possible to give cavity nesters and bark drillers breeding and feeding sites. If possible, leave leaf litter so that ground-dwelling species and those that hunt for insects and mollusks on the forest floor will have this resource.

Shade and sun. The open areas of your garden will attract birds who feel comfortable in the open, rather than in leaf shade. But if there are no trees in your yard, don't expect to lure shade-loving species of birds.

Weeds. Many birds are much more attracted to weed seeds than to tame garden plants, and an out-of-sight corner allowed to grow wild will be popular with birds. Gathering weed seeds is a fall project and one that is especially good for children. Gather seeds in fields and by the roadside by stripping handfuls of grass seeds and seeds of other desirable wild plants into a paper bag. Plant the seeds in a bed that is specially turned over for this purpose, but beware: In the "burbs," your neighbors may become incensed if your delightful weeds suddenly sprout in the middle of their perennial borders and zoysia grass.

Fruit. Plants and shrubs that have berries when the weather is cold will attract large numbers of birds. Birds love to eat berries of japonica, cotoneaster, berberis, holly, rowan, hawthorn, pyracantha, stranvaesia, cherry, and viburnum. Can you offer an arbor that will eventually have enough grapes for both you and the birds to enjoy? It also helps to leave as many spent blossoms on plants as possible so that their seeds will ripen and provide much-appreciated bird food.

Flowers. Here is a list of annual and perennial plants that will provide flowers and seeds for birds: quaking grass (*Briza maxima*), love grass (*Eragrostis tef*), hare's tail (*Lagurus ovatus*), crimson fountain (*Pennisetum setaceum*), plains bristle grass (*Setaria macrostachya*), amaranthus (*Amaranthus* sp.), sunflower (*Helianthus*), California poppy (*Eschscholzia californica*), love-in-a-mist (*Nigella damascena*), pink (*Dianthus*), zinnia (*Zinnia*), aster (*Aster*), purple coneflower (*Echinacea purpurea*), scabiosa (*Scabiosa spectabile*), globe thistle (*Echinacea*), coreopsis (*Coreopsis*), butterfly flower (*Asclepias tuberosa*), black-eyed Susan (*Rudbeckia*), statice (*Limonium latifolium*), and showy stonecrop (*Sedum spectabile*).

Let a corner of your yard grow wild and reap the rewards in the diversity of birds who will become your neighbors. Here, an indigo bunting perches on nodding thistle. In autumn, buntings, chickadees, and goldfinches will harvest a treat of thistle seeds.

Shoe-box gardens. Do not worry if your space is limited. Thanks to container gardening, there are still many options open to you. The following plants can be grown in containers to attract birds: Japanese maple (*Acer palmatum*), boxwood (*Boxus*), cherry laurel (*Prunus laurocerasus* "otto luyken"), Chinese holly (*Ilex cornuta*), Japanese holly (*Ilex crenata*), yaupon (*Ilex vomitoria* "Nana"), juniper (*Juniperus*), mugo pine (*Pinus mugo* var. *mugo* "Compacta"), myrtle (*Myrtus communis*), and yew (*Taxus*, all species, dwarf cultivars).

A male rose-breasted grosbeak and flowering apple tree go hand in hand.

Radical lawn. This idea is not for everyone—or for everyone's neighborhood—but it would be a great idea to stop mowing the lawn for a few months in the spring or early summer and see what grows. You will probably see a whole variety of wildflowers—even some unusual or possibly rare ones, depending upon where you live. To reassure the neighbors that your raggedy meadow is intentional, mow a graceful path through it and make sure that the edges of the path are especially clear-cut. In late July, harvest your lawn-meadow. Rake up the hay and add it to your compost pile. If you want to spice up your meadow, you might buy potted meadow wildflowers and plant them among the grasses.

© Skip Moody/Dembinsky Photo Associates

Composites such as these cultivated stiff asters (above) and wild black-eyed Susans (below) provide meadows where a variety of insects—and the birds that eat them—can thrive.

© Richard Day

CHAPTER SIX

North American Bird-Feeding Year

JANUARY

Only the hardiest feathered species—jays, chickadees, woodpeckers, juncos, cardinals, titmice, nuthatches, sparrows, and starlings—brave winter's coldest days and depend upon your backyard feeder to give them abundant high-energy food. Suet is a must in these bitter January days, and wet water will disappear down those parched little throats almost as fast as you can offer it.

Days are short and nights are long. Snowbirds gather in flocks to feast on your grain; at night, the great horned owl (*Bubo virginianus*) hoots, defining a fierce territorial boundary. Snowbirds feed in flocks; your breath steams in the air. We are deep into winter. Blue jays (*Cyanocitta cristata*) seem twice as vividly blue, and northern cardinals (*Cardinalis cardinalis*) are brilliant red against the snow. Tiny downy woodpeckers (*Picoides pubescens*) are a crisp black and white, with the caps of the males a vibrant blood red.

Evening grosbeaks (*Coccothraustes vespertinus*) are the prize winter birds. These finches descend in large, nomadic flocks, especially to feeders that offer sunflower seeds. To increase your chances of attracting them, you should plan ahead. When the maples shed their seeds in late spring and early summer, rake and dry a quantity of these, and store them until winter comes. Offer maple seeds on your platform feeder along with sunflower seeds. Garden trees that evening grosbeaks prefer include maples, spruces, firs, and box elders.

Listen to the birds before you get out of bed on a cold morning—or better yet, lie in bed, sip hot coffee, and listen to the birds. Record the dawn chorus: It shouldn't be more than call notes and twitters; most birds won't sing their territorial songs until stimulated by the longer days of spring.

It's gray squirrel mating season. Look for a line of squirrels racing through the treetops or squirrels chasing up and down tree trunks. The first squirrel in the line will probably be a female in breeding condition, followed by several avidly interested males. With a delicate turn of phrase, Hal Borland once

Evening grosbeaks travel in large, loose wintering flocks and can appear in numbers overnight to the delight of the backyard-bird feeder.

A cardinal livens the winter scene.

© George E. Stewart/Dembinsky Photo Associates

Puffed up against the cold, a tufted titmouse perches on one foot while warming the other within his down coat. When wild foods are frozen or snow-covered, food in backyard feeders can aid in the survival of individual birds.

wrote that "young squirrels are nurtured in acorn cups." But, in your yard, if your squirrel defenses aren't up, this season's babies will be nurtured on your birdseed!

FEBRUARY

On February 2, Groundhog Day, Americans watch for the weather prophecy from woodchucks. Whatever the groundhogs decide, however, there are still six weeks of winter ahead according to the calendar. February is winter's turning point.

Great horned owls (*Bubo virginianus*) are nesting now, and their territorial calls are loud and eerie. Barred owls (*Strix varia*) start calling now, too, even though they won't be mating until March. When the snow falls, think of the big owls, warming their eggs and nestlings in the starlit treetops.

© George E. Stewart/Dembinsky Photo Associates

To some, the call of the barred owl sounds like "Who cooks for you? Who cooks for you? Who cooks for you allll?" Owls call from dusk to dawn and can sometimes be heard on gloomy, overcast spring days.

At your ground feeder, white-throated sparrows (*Zonotrichia albicollis*), song sparrows (*Melospiza melodia*), and field sparrows (*Spizella pusilla*) flutter and feed, if the house sparrows (*Passer domesticus*) haven't crowded them out of your neighborhood. Listen for the song of the white-throated sparrow: a clear, whistled "Poor Sam Peabody-Peabody-Peabody." At this season, it is often fragmented so that you may hear only "Poor Sam" or "Peabody" or only the last, repetitious phrase.

© John Gerlach/Dembinsky Photo Associates

Distinctively striped white-throated sparrows breed in the far north. They are among the earliest migrants, and their calls herald the transition from winter to spring.

If you aren't good at identifying sparrows and instead call any little bird by that name, now is the time to get the binoculars and the bird book and learn better. Look for the white-striped head and yellow dot on the inner corner of the eye of the white-throated sparrow. A sparrow with a streaky breast with a dark central dot is a song sparrow. Male house sparrows have a gray cap, chestnut eye patch, and a distinctive black chin and bib, while females are much more drab. Male field sparrows have a bright rusty cap and a pink bill, while their look-alike cousins, chipping sparrows (*Spizella passerina*), have a similar rusty cap, but a white line over the eye and a black line through it. They don't have a pink bill, either.

Look for another winter prize at your feeder among your sparrows: pine siskins (*Carduelis pinus*). They look like streaky, rather nondescript little birds, but the males have a bit of yellow on the wings and at the base of the tail. Watch for the yellow, especially when a flock of sparrows takes flight.

Watch behavior at your feeder. Which birds are aggressive and dominate the feeder, threatening other birds? Which ones are placid and sweet-natured, feeding in flocks and small groups?

Is there anything more energetic than a chickadee (*Parus atricapillus*) at a feeder? And what an appetite: A chickadee must eat its weight in food each winter's day. These ever-hungry fluffballs are another reason to keep your feeders full in winter, even if it means a second trip outside. Start listening to the chickadees in the early mornings. When do they stop repeating "Chickadee-dee-dee" and start singing a sweet "Phoe-be, Phoe-be"?

Nuthatches of all three species (white-breasted, red-breasted, and the minute brown-headed [*Sitta carolinensis*, *S. canadensis*, and *S. pusilla*]) spiral around tree trunks and limbs, gleaning insects from crevices in the bark. Downy and hairy woodpeckers (*Picoides pubescens* and *P. villosus*) dig juicy grubs from beneath bark. Both will visit suet feeders, so now is the time to offer your suet concoctions, crammed into pinecones, feeder sticks, and feeder logs as well as in wire cages attached to tree trunks and in suet bags suspended from tree limbs.

Male northern cardinals whistle a series of clear notes and females respond. The call is most often given as "whoit-whoit-whoit," but some of my clever students say it sounds like a video-game sound effect. When you hear it repeated again and again before being varied, you can surmise that a pair of cardinals has taken up territory in your backyard. Most folks think that only male birds sing, and while this is true of many species, both male and female cardinals sing equally well. Even more interesting, they sing duets,

White-breasted nuthatches are year-round residents in many states. They land head downward on tree trunks and spiral down and around searching for insects that hide in the crevices of the bark. All three species of nuthatches are frequent feeder visitors who are especially fond of sunflower seeds.

technically called countersinging. If a pair of cardinals visits your feeder, watch carefully to see mate feeding, when a male offers a seed or other bit of food to a female.

Osier dogwood stems are turning red; maple sap is beginning to rise; alder bushes attract early pollinating bees.

MARCH

March sees the first spring flowers: skunk cabbage, whose green-and-purple-hooded flowers smell like rotting meat. Grass begins to green up, and pussy willows wink from streamsides. Male red-winged blackbirds (*Agelaius phoeniceus*) return from their southern wintering grounds and set up territories. Buzzards return to Hinckley, Ohio, on March 15. Swallows return to San Juan Capistrano, California, on March 19.

© John Mielcarek/Dembinsky Photo Associates

Robins spend the winter in large flocks that assemble in early autumn and disperse in early spring. Flocking robins are quieter than territorial birds. They seldom sing the typical robin caroling song at this time of year; instead, their robin "flicker" call can be heard.

Thaws begin, and worms appear on your sidewalk after a heavy rain. One day in March, your lawn will be alive with dozens of robins (*Turdus migratorius*) who have returned from their southern winter. Now is the time to note the changes in the dawn chorus. Robins bring the spring; things are going to get busy from here on out. Male robins have ruddier and brighter orange breasts than females, who look washed out in comparison. You'll seldom be able to lure robins to your feeder (although you might want to try with bits of stale bread), but they will love your birdbath, may take some oyster shell and grit, and will nest in your evergreen trees and feast in your pyracantha and mulberries.

© John Gerlach/Dembinsky Photo Associates

Among the handsomest of birds, purple finches are seed eaters.

Winds of spring pick up; hepaticas, violets, spring beauties, and wind flowers appear; willows become amber blond. Plush catkins stud pussy willows. Mourning-cloak butterflies, newly emerged from winter sleep, flaunt their wide, brown wings, edged with pale yellow, dotted with tiny blue. This is our common first butterfly.

Shrill calls of spring peepers resound from roadside ponds and ditches; wood frogs cluck and chuckle in still woodland waters. Purple finches and house finches (*Carpodacus purpureus* and *C. mexicanus*) may arrive at your feeder in record numbers drawn to black-oil sunflower seed, canary seed, and thistle. They prefer to feed on platform feeders that are high off the ground. Fox and song sparrows begin singing; bluebirds become numerous and begin singing and nesting; cowbirds arrive.

© Jim Battles/Dembinsky Photo Associates

House wrens are tiny, lively insect eaters who like to build nests in the holes of dead trees. If they nest in your backyard, listen to these birds scold as you approach their territory.

© Gary Crandall/Envision

Mountain bluebirds are found in the western United States, and like their eastern relatives, they are threatened by competition for nesting cavities from European starlings.

© John Gerlach/Dembinsky Photo Associates

The short days of spring help bring great blue herons into breeding condition. The mutual display shown here is thought to reinforce the bond between mates and help them be more successful parents.

APRIL

By the end of March, your birdhouses should be completely refurbished, cleaned, and hung, ready for the migrants to inspect and, hopefully, occupy. House wrens (*Troglodytes aedon*) appear the first week in April. You may be able to attract them to your platform feeder with suet, white-bread crumbs, or corn bread. Put up a wren house and prepare to be scolded.

Purple trillium, trailing arbutus, dutchman's breeches, and shad bush blossom in the woodlands. Clouds of dogwood blossoms drift amid leafless trees. Maples are crimson in swampy places as marsh marigold spreads a yellow carpet below.

Duck migration is in full northward swing in the early weeks of April. Herons and kingfishers usually appear in the first week. Then look for fox sparrows, purple martins, bank swallows, brown thrashers, and the earliest warblers. By the end of April, bird-watchers are glued to their binoculars as gorgeous warblers begin to fill the trees. Hummingbirds, kingbirds, vireos, wood thrushes, and veeries have flown into breeding territory. All these birds will flock to your garden if you have plenty of edge habitat as well as berries and insects for them.

Crows and small owls nest in April. Crows usually have nests and eggs by April 15; think about that while you're sending your annual love letter to the IRS.

MAY

May is the height of the spring bird migration, and each species' movements are coordinated to coincide with the appearance of the foods that they and their young will eat on their nesting grounds. The dawn

© Wendy Shattil, Robert Rozinski/Tom Stack and Associates

Broad-tailed hummingbirds are common west of the Rocky Mountains. They look nearly identical to eastern ruby-throated hummingbirds, but they don't sound the same. The wings of broad-tails whistle with a metallic sound, while those of ruby-throats make a mellow hum.

© Gary Meszaros/Dembinsky Photo Associates

Insectivorous black-throated green warblers will never visit your feeder and aren't common at birdbaths, but you can entice them into your yard by planting large trees such as oaks whose spring tassels (strings of flowers) will draw the insects that warblers feed upon.

chorus is now filled with fluent, exuberant songs. Your resident birds will act as magnets for seed-eating migrants who fly by your neighborhood. Your garden plantings will do the rest of the work of attracting them and will afford you glimpses of insect-eating species who will never come to your feeders; black-throated blue warblers, blackburnian warblers, and black-and-white warblers are only three examples.

Migrants travel mainly at night, and it isn't at all unusual to wake up on a May morning and find the previously birdless branches alive with flickering, twittering, hungry warblers. They will loiter in your trees and bushes through the day and then push northward again at night if the weather is fair.

Now is the time to begin offering nesting material, either from your platform feeder or tied in bunches to branches. It may help you lure species that otherwise wouldn't approach a feeder.

It's also the time to begin sleuthing about your property to see who's nesting and where. And at the same time, begin urging your friends who have outdoor cats to trim their cat's claws and tie a bell on the relentlessly stalking hunter if they won't keep their pet inside. The annual losses of billions of songbirds to cat predation from *well-fed* domestic felines are only now beginning to be recognized as another of the incredibly shortsighted effects of our "civilization."

This is the time when many people take down their bird feeders, some because they will be going away on vacation soon, others because they think it won't be good for the birds to leave them up. Birds who are defending territory and nesting need food now more than at any other time. So keep those feeders filled! If you're going away, ask another bird enthusiast to mind the store while you're on vacation. Remember to fill your suet feeders with peanut-butter gorp, which won't melt or go rancid as the weather warms.

You can visit birds at their nests if you are very cautious and quiet in your movements. If you stay still, the birds will calm down and forget your presence after a while and go about the business of feeding those hungry chicks. If a parent becomes too alarmed and stays away from its young for more than five minutes, you must leave the area immediately, so that you don't frighten the bird into abandoning the nest.

© George E. Stewart/Dembinsky Photo Associates

The common yellow throat is a warbler that prefers lots of low-growing cover. Listen for its "witchety-witchety" song and look for it in raspberry thickets, in lower branches of trees and shrubs, and as pictured here, at the edges of marshes.

© Jeffrey Rich

The intense orange color of northern orioles is always a delightful surprise. Here, a member of the western race, bullock's oriole, feeds on an insect.

Oaks are in tassel now, attracting many insects and insect-eating birds. Oaks are warbler magnets, and on a fine day, there is nothing more enjoyable than settling back into an observation post (preferably the laid-back way, by lying flat on your back with a pillow under your head) and scanning the crown of an oak or tulip tree for warblers.

Apples and lilacs are in blossom and suddenly northern orioles (*Icterus galbula*) are here, flaming in the treetops. Try to draw them to your feeder with orange slices—some say this doesn't work—or try a shot glass of orange juice. Orioles like to nest in elms and will weave their beautiful, pendulous nest creations with bakery string if you offer it. Collect many colors of bakery string, tie them in four-inch (10cm) lengths, and see what your orioles prefer. Imagine the tropical-color contrasts: a hot orange oriole peering out of a lime green nest! Improbable, but still possible.

Late April or early May is the time to put up the hummingbird feeder. Keep it up and filled with freshly brewed nectar (discard after the second day or else the birds will be feeding on alcoholic sugar water).

© Claude Steelman/Tom Stack and Associates

A female black-chinned hummingbird hovers at a columbine. While there is only one species of hummingbird in most eastern states, the western United States has fifteen species of hummingbird that will visit feeders and are especially attracted to bright-colored flowers, making hummingbird gardening an achievable goal and a rewarding hobby.

JUNE

Chimney swifts (*Chaetura pelagica*) are back in June, and if you're lucky, a flight may take up residence in your chimney, drawn again by the insects you've cultivated in your bird garden. Their "twinkling" flight will make you glad you don't use commercial pesticides in your garden.

© Steve & Dave Maslowski

American goldfinches seem to be calling "Potato chip, potato chip" as they fly to feeders such as this thistle feeder full of Niger thistle seed. One added benefit of feeding the birds is that the calls and songs of resident birds will become familiar. When exotic migrants pass through, one is more apt to notice them because their calls and songs are different from those of winter and year-round residents.

Chokecherries bloom at roadsides, planted by the birds who love to eat those berries that make your mouth pucker. The main bird migration is over, and woods and gardens become quiet as the birds settle down to nest and raise their broods.

American goldfinches (*Carduelis tristis*) are a bright dash of black and yellow as they bob over the fields. They are the summer prize at your feeder, your reward for offering black-oil sunflower seed, thistle seed, and hulled sunflower seed, and especially for letting those thistles grow in your weed corner. Goldfinches love to bathe and will be attracted to your birdbath.

A new generation of birds begins to appear at your feeder in mid-June, brought there by your faithful clients who no doubt have told their fledglings that they know of this great little place to grab a bite.

Look for baby robins on the lawn as they watch their parents listen for worms and then gape, crouch, flutter their wings, and screech to be stuffed with the worm dangling so deliciously from their parent's bill.

Mid-June marks the beginning of flight school; all over the garden fledglings try their wings. And, as though timed perfectly to coincide with all these new young mouths that must be fed, blackberries, raspberries, black caps, and many other wild fruits ripen, ready to be harvested by the birds.

JULY

Tree swallows (*Iridoprocne bicolor*) begin flocking on the marshes now, preparing to migrate, while the goldfinches may now be laying their first eggs. The hatching of their young is timed to coincide with the ripening of grass and thistle seeds.

© MacDonald Photography/Envision

Parent birds cannot resist the demands of these tiny, wide-open, begging beaks.

July is a continuation of June. Because there are so many wild foods ripening, there will be fewer birds at your feeder. But, if you are lucky, some of these will be baby bluebirds, baby cardinals, and young chickadees. You will be able to watch their first splashings in your birdbath—truly a comic delight.

Keep those hummingbird feeders filled with freshly brewed nectar and hanging in the shade.

Your summer garden should be filled with bird flowers; wild bergamot, purple coneflower, red columbine, scarlet sage, trumpet honeysuckle, petunia, phlox, lilies, trumpet creeper, tree tobacco, fuchsia, jewelweed, eucalyptus, and century plant will all attract hummingbirds.

AUGUST

Goldenrod comes into bloom this month as midsummer draws to a height. Birds have almost stopped singing altogether; the dawn chorus is mere notes and chips that only the best-trained ears can identify.

Your birdbath will be popular on August afternoons as the birds crowd the rim, each waiting a turn to duck and splash. If you are religious about cleaning and filling it each morning and if your drip bucket is working, your yard should still be popular with birds, who have many natural foods to eat.

© John Mielcarek/Dembinsky Photo Associates

The immaculate white underparts of this tree swallow contrast with its green-blue cap, wings, and back. Tree swallows will nest in boxes and provide you with mosquito-removal services free of charge.

Northern migrants, birds who bypassed your region to settle farther north to breed in boreal forests and on tundra, begin to appear as they make their way south for the winter. Look for baybreasted and blackburnian warblers in the second week, Nashville and magnolia warblers in the third week.

Tree swallows and rough-winged swallows begin to leave for the south all this month.

SEPTEMBER

September is the month of fruits, squirrels feeding on mushrooms, beech mast, deer antlers, winter pelts on woodchucks, and bird migration. Watch for gathering flocks of redwings and other blackbirds over open fields and marshes.

If you haven't been feeding the birds all summer, now is the time to refurbish the feeder and lay in a new store of feed for the winter.

Wait for two weeks after you've seen the last hummer to take down the hummingbird feeders, because there may still be birds flying in from the north who may find your feeder. Some people worry about disrupting the natural migratory movements of hummingbirds by leaving their feeders up for two extra weeks in this way, but hummingbirds are ill designed to endure the rigors of a northern winter, and because they are a product of natural selection and evolution, they know when to fly south, and will.

OCTOBER

October is the month of color in the woods. Hickory, walnut, pecan, beechnuts, acorns, and even some chestnuts ripen, providing all seed eaters with a rich feast and nuts to stow away for winter's cold.

Swallows depart from San Juan Capistrano, California, this month, and the birds who remain are those who can feed on seeds and fruit.

Look for bird families feeding together: robins, bluebirds, chickadees, house finches.

Weeds and grasses are ripening their seeds now, giving seed eaters fuel for the winter.

© Rob Simpson

Northern rough-winged swallows have a distinctive brown back, throat, and breast. These birds nest in burrows on riverbanks or along streams, and like all swallows, they feed on flying insects.

© John Mielcarek/Dembinsky Photo Associates

Put up a feeder and sooner or later exuberant chickadees will visit. Listen for their "Phoe-be" call—it's a sure sign that either spring or autumn is coming. Their "chick-a-dee" song is more characteristic of summer and winter.

© Diana L. Stratton/Tom Stack and Associates

Shown here on a cliff face in Yellowstone Park, these cliff swallows are nesting on a rounded mound of mud they've built, which is characteristic of all swallows' nests. This species of swallow migrates to San Juan Capistrano each year.

© R. Revels/Royal Society for the Protection of Birds

A European starling is quite beautiful in its spotty winter plumage. Even though starlings are aggressive, they can be entertaining. Watch their "wind-up starling" display at a nest site, and listen to their repertoire of whistles and odd sounds.

Your backyard nesting birds have departed, and now is the time to take down and refurbish your bird houses. If necessary, take the time to shop for new ones or, if you're a do-it-yourselfer, order plans and make new ones. While you're at it, think about a bluebird trail. All it takes is a string of nest boxes, which you'll need to check once a week to evict any pest birds and see how the bluebirds are doing. Bluebirds prefer their nests four feet (120cm) off the ground; boxes on top of fence posts are excellent. Bluebirds need your help with nest boxes because tree cavities are at a premium in most neighborhoods. Think about it: How many of your neighbors have standing dead trees or dead tree stumps on their property? How many do you have? Moreover, many tree cavities are occupied by raucous bands of aggressive starlings (*Sturnus vulgaris*) or cheeky house sparrows, which are widely considered to be pest birds. Your string of nest boxes, with openings designed to admit bluebirds and restrict starlings and house sparrows, could help bring the

© Susan Day

Because of its small entrance, this nest box favors eastern bluebirds and discourages the starlings and house sparrows that monopolize natural cavities.

bluebird back to your neighborhood. Write the North American Bluebird Society (chapter 3, page 53) for more information.

Now is the time to put away any birdbaths that will be damaged by cold and replace them with more durable ones. It's also the time to think about how you're going to offer the birds water in cold weather.

NOVEMBER

November is a mix of winter and summer that can be as harsh or as mild as unpredictable March.

Bird migrations continue. Sea ducks go south in the first two weeks of the month, phoebes in the first week, and redwings, which have been staging for their migration by gathering in large, nervous flocks, will disappear by the third week. Many of the sparrows—fox, song, swamp, vesper, and chipping—will go south this month, and the winter visitors begin to arrive from the north, depending upon local weather conditions.

© Rod Planck/Dembinsky Photo Associates

Across the northern third of the United States and southern Canada, snow buntings (above) are synonymous with winter. The males of this species of sparrow are white and black in breeding season. All that remains of this distinctive plumage when these birds fly south for the winter are large white wing patches. As you might expect, the male's wings are larger than those of the female. Common redpolls (below) thrive in open spaces and are usually seen hunting for seeds in snow-covered, weedy fields across the northern United States and Canada. The male has a red cap and breast, while only the female's cap is red.

DECEMBER

Winter residents visit your feeder now, and it's especially important to keep the feeders filled after a storm, when all the natural foods will be covered with drifts.

This is the season to watch for rarities in your bird garden. Bohemian waxwings, northern shrikes, redpolls, crossbills, snow buntings, Lapland longspurs, and horned larks are all possible.

Now's the time when backyard-bird feeding is at its coziest: Your feeders are filled, water is ready for the birds, the suet is out, and the birds are settling down to feed. Shut the door on the wind that sweeps in from the north and stamp the snow off your boots. It's time to settle into your favorite chair with your binoculars and a warm drink, put your feet up, and enjoy the birds that you've earned all year long.

© John Gerlach/Tom Stack and Associates

CHAPTER SEVEN

Squirrels: Foiling the Archenemy

"I used to like to feed the birds," my friend Connie said as we were pulling into her tree-shaded drive. "But when it ended up that all I was really feeding was squirrels, I quit!" This battle is waged every day in millions of backyards, all over the world. Think of all those squirrels. Some may be sleeping curled up in their leafy nests or snug in leaf-lined dens in old tree holes, but wherever they are and probably even while they sleep, those active, whirring little minds are consumed with one thought: how to steal your birdseed. There's no doubt about it: Once you put up a bird feeder, you have made the opening salvo in the eternal war against the squirrels.

FORMIDABLE FOE

Squirrels are worthy opponents, endowed with powers and abilities far beyond those of lesser mammals—like you and me. They are Olympic-class high jumpers and can clear four feet (1.2m) vertically—the equivalent of a six-foot (1.8m) human springing thirty-two feet (9.6m) into the air. Imagine one backyard-bird feeder watching in frustration as a squirrel raced the entire length of a deck railing at top speed and launched itself twenty feet (6m) through the air—all for the sake of a little birdseed! Squirrels can climb anything except glass. They can easily scamper up brick, aluminum siding, or any vertical surface, and this is the reason you don't want to hang a feeder from your roof—or closer than eight feet (2.4m) from any potential squirrel launchpad. And remember, virtually everything in your backyard falls into this category.

If their leaping abilities weren't enough, squirrels' teeth and cleverly designed paws allow them to seize and gnaw through almost anything. Squirrels love to gnaw, and indeed, like all rodents, they must gnaw to

Chickadee versus squirrel: Even a metal cage cannot protect suet from the gnawing of a determined and hungry squirrel.

keep their ever-growing incisor teeth in working order. If they are fed an exclusively soft diet or if an incisor is lost, depriving its mate of a matching grinding surface, the teeth will inexorably grow and curve inward, and eventually the palate and braincase will be pierced and the squirrel will die. This grisly death is a rare occurrence; most often it's your plastic squirrel baffle, plastic sunflower-seed feeder, or wooden bird feeder that gets gnawed and destroyed. Hungry squirrels will consume plastic-coated wire; many metals will deter them, but some soft aluminum baffles succumb easily when attacked by a hungry squirrel.

© Gay Bumgarner/Photo/Nats

Baby squirrels are cute and easily tamed; juveniles are adorably curious and frisky. Squirrels can make interesting pets until they begin to sexually mature; then their territorial tantrums and sharp teeth can become both frightening and dangerous.

GOLDEN RULES FOR SQUIRREL DETERRENCE

1. Be prepared: Baffle every feeder.
2. The bigger the baffle, the better. Raccoons and cats like bird feeders, too.
3. Know that if you hang a feeder from a tree, sooner or later a squirrel will take over.
4. Never put a bird feeder on a fence.
5. If your neighborhood is Squirrel City, use only baffled, pole-mounted feeders that are at least ten feet (3m) from any squirrel launch site.
6. Spike pole grease with cayenne pepper and give would-be raiders a fiery mouthful that may remind them to stay away.
7. Buy only Lexan or other polycarbonate plastic feeders. Squirrels will probably eventually get to these, too, but they'll protect your seed longer than other feeders.
8. Remove perches from tubular feeders. The birds don't need them, and they give squirrels an easy hold on your feeder.

Courtesy of Hendon Squirrels/Photography by Martin Ancketill/Hampstead Heath, London

When a squirrel jumps onto this feeder, the green tube slides down, hiding the birdseed and scooting the squirrel down onto the ground, thereby protecting the seed.

SQUIRREL-PROOF FEEDERS

You may want to invest in metal squirrel-proof feeders that have ungnawable metal doors that swing down, preventing anything that weighs as much as a squirrel from raiding your feeders. My objection to these bird feeders is that they don't have the homey, friendly look of most feeders, but instead look like military bunkers. However, if you want or need to be this aggressive, you may want to investigate these rather expensive pole-mounted metal feeders.

There are more graceful-looking feeders that claim to be squirrel-proof. The usual design is plastic-coated metal mesh that sheathes a Lexan tubular feeder. The seed ports of these feeders are surrounded by metal and the perches are metal, too. These work because the metal around the seed ports prevents the squirrels from gnawing on the ports, enlarging them and spilling the seed onto the ground, while the metal mesh keeps paws and teeth from reaching into the seed ports. Squirrels are unbelievably clever and hardworking, though, and it's probably only a matter of time before they figure out a way to break into this feeder design. My bird-feeding guru, however, who lives in a squirrel-infested neighborhood in a small Wisconsin lakeside community, has had a feeder up without a baffle for two years and her squirrels haven't broken in yet.

© Richard Day

This triple tube feeder equipped with a squirrel baffle offers good protection from overhead attack. If it is hung far from any possible launch pad, it should be fairly squirrel-proof.

© C. H. Gomersall/Royal Society for the Protection of Birds

A cage of plastic-coated wire (above) will protect a feeder from squirrel attack, but it may trap and panic small birds who may be unable to find their way out of the holes once they have squeezed inside. Use a design like this with caution. A pole-mounted squirrel foiler (below left) should keep the rodents out of the birdseed. This feeder (below right) may be inelegant and ugly, but it is practical and beautiful to someone who's beseiged by squirrels. If the baffle is mounted so that squirrels can't stretch around it or jump on top of it, it just might work.

© Richard Day

© Richard Day

CHAPTER EIGHT

Answers to Common Backyard-Bird Problems

Having plotted strategy against those formidable, bushy-tailed opponents otherwise known as squirrels (see the previous chapter), it is time to deal with some of the other most commonly encountered nuisances and dilemmas associated with backyard-bird feeding. Although it is easy to become discouraged when obstacles arise, do not let these hindrances deprive you of the pleasures of feeding and observing birds. Most problems have simple solutions that require only a minimal amount of effort, so do not give up your bird-feeding activities. You'll find that the joys of backyard-bird feeding by far outweigh the inconveniences that may occur during the course of this rewarding pastime.

Here are some of the most common problems that backyard-bird lovers are faced with. By following the suggested solutions, you will be helping both yourself and your feathered friends.

BACKYARD-BIRD PROBLEMS AND SOLUTIONS

1. The only birds that come to my feeder are grackles, house sparrows, crows, and starlings. How can I get rid of them and attract pretty birds like goldfinches and indigo buntings?

This common problem can often be solved by offering Niger seed (also called thistle seed) in a feeder specially designed to exclude larger birds such as grackles, crows, and starlings. Thistle seed is a big favorite with many species of small, colorful finches, and once they discover it, they will become thistle feeder regulars. To ensure that the birds you want to attract won't be frightened away by more aggressive species, such as blackbirds and crows, hang your thistle feeder at least fifteen to twenty feet (4.5 to 6m) from any other feeders, or remove the feeder that attracts the larger species. If the undesired species continue to be a problem, try offering different mixes of seeds until you hit on the blend that discourages the unwanted birds. If you live in an urban setting, there may be few colorful finches around. Be patient: It may be a long time before those few individuals in your neighborhood locate your feeder.

2. A hawk just attacked the birds at my feeder! What should I do?

If this happens in your backyard, you'll probably feel upset and somewhat responsible. Try to minimize these feelings by considering that predator and prey populations have evolved together for millions of years; what you may have just witnessed is a natural drama that is essential for the health and success of both predator and prey populations. Just as your treasured backyard bird regulars have young to feed, so do predatory birds, and all species have important ecological roles to play. Although it is natural to become disheartened when a hawk swoops down and seizes one of the birds you have come to cherish, do not become so discouraged that you take down your feeders in an attempt to keep other feathered favorites from being killed. Instead, try to take a broader look at the situation: Both predators and prey have hungry chicks to nourish, and by continuing to feed your backyard birds, you are contributing to the well-being of all the species in the local food web.

Predation at bird feeders is a rare occurrence, but if a hawk does become a regular visitor at your bird feeder, you need to relocate the feeder so that unwary, hungry birds are not such easy targets for passing predators. Try to screen a feeder beneath overhanging foliage, but avoid high bushes where house cats can lie in wait for ground-feeding species.

3. Neighborhood children have just appeared at my door with a baby bird that has fallen out of its nest. Knowing that I feed birds, they expect me to take care of this one. What should I do?

First of all, try to avoid this responsibility. It is nearly impossible for a mere human to duplicate the care and

© Richard Day

Here, American goldfinches and pine siskins dine at a thistle feeder. If the more aggressive house finches are abundant in your backyard and you wish to reserve thistle seed for chickadees, titmice, and goldfinches, there is a variation of this feeder that allows birds to feed only if they're hanging upside down. This is a nearly impossible acrobatic feat for house finches, but chickadees, titmice, and goldfinches do it all the time.

© Richard Day

Common grackles, who often monopolize feeders, are handsome but aggressive relatives of crows and blackbirds. Flocks of these birds are intriguing to watch as they flit across a corn field, gleaning spilled grain, but in your backyard they can become messy, noisy pests who ravenously raid your bird feeder. If an unwanted winter roost appears in your backyard, remove your feeders. These birds will quickly move on when the food is gone.

© Hugh P. Smith, Jr.

Is this sharp-shinned hawk waiting for dinner, or did "dinner" just fly away?

feeding program of the average avian parent. Not only do we have limited supplies of live insects and appropriate seed mixes in our refrigerators, but we are usually unable to duplicate the correct care routine and feeding schedule known only to parent birds. So, no matter how much patience you have or how adept you are at raising domestic animals, you simply do not have the skills necessary to assume the role of bird parent. In some instances you may be able to raise a bird to the fledgling stage and eventually see it fly free, but its ability to find a mate of its own species may be impaired because it will have imprinted on a human as a nestling. Also, the bird could die from a vitamin deficiency disease caused by the lack of proper nutrition it received during its developmental stages. All things considered, it is best to avoid becoming a bird parent in the first place.

This course of action may sound heartless, especially when you look at a shuddering, squawking, helpless nestling bird. However, adult birds of the same species, who are better equipped than you to care for the young bird, will also be unable to resist its helpless and demanding behaviors. In most cases, if the nestling is taken back to the place where it was found, its cries will attract its parents or another adult bird who will assume parental duties toward it. Thus, you are probably doing the young bird a favor by not adopting the role of parent yourself.

If possible, you should replace the bird in its nest, retreat to a safe distance, and wait for the parents to appear. Don't worry that the parents will kill the bird or desert the nest because it "smells like people." Most birds rely on vision, not olfaction, as their primary sense. Indeed, most birds have a poorly developed

© Robert Lankinen/The Wildlife Collection

Although "abandoned" nestlings can sometimes be raised successfully by humans, this difficult and demanding task is best left to parent birds. Most nestlings are fed a diet that is similar to what they will eat as adults. For example, this male goldfinch feeds his young a regurgitated blend of seeds.

© Richard Day

"Look, and make it quick" should be your motto if you happen to find a nest with a young bird in it. Keep in mind that one of the parents is probably hiding nearby, anxiously waiting for you to leave; if you stay too long, it is likely the parent bird will abandon the nest and young. In addition, your curiosity may lead dogs, cats, and other predators to the nest.

sense of smell. Unlike mammals, they do not seem to be bothered by the human scent that will be all over the nestling bird. If you cannot replace the bird within the nest, put it on the ground directly below. Keep yourself hidden and watch out for predators (squirrels, house cats, dogs, and other birds such as crows, grackles, and hawks). If any of these threatening creatures arrive, frighten them away from the vulnerable baby bird.

If the parent birds do not appear after twenty or thirty minutes, you may have to assume the role of parent yourself. In this case, call a local zoo or raptor rehabilitation center for specific advice on how to care for your bird. Until you learn the correct approximation of its diet (which varies from species to species), feed it dry dog food or cat food that has been softened in milk. Place a morsel of food about the size of a dried green pea on the end of a pencil eraser, and gently push the food down into the throat of the begging bird. Keep the nestling warm with a heating pad or hot water bottle. Good luck.

4. At the end of each bird-feeding season there is a huge mound of rotting hulls and seeds beneath my bird feeder. This awful mess kills my grass and requires a lot of cleaning up. How can I eliminate this problem?

There are several ways to approach this situation; one of the following suggestions should work for you.

A. Many stores that specialize in bird-feeding supplies (see chapter 3, page 52) offer a wasteless seed (usually composed exclusively of sunflower-seed hearts) that will take care of this problem completely. The drawback of this solution is the higher cost of the seed, but before you eliminate it on account of expense, consider the value of the hours you will save by not having to clean up all those wasted seeds and grass-killing sunflower-seed hulls. Also, consider the joy of feeding a seed that does not damage the grass beneath the feeder. If you are a lawn fanatic who is proud of an even span of green turf, or if you have a tiny and thus highly valuable lawn, this method may be best for you.

B. Try digging up the turf beneath the feeder, setting down a large (at least four feet [1.2m] in diameter) circle of black plastic sheeting, and covering it with a thick layer of crushed stone or paving it with bricks or irregular slates. When using this method, keep in mind that the smoother the surface, the easier it will be to clean.

C. A similar idea is to landscape the area beneath your feeder with low bushes to hide the feeder mess. This method will work as long as you keep the feeder out of the range of predators and those ever-present, seed-stealing squirrels.

D. Garden supply and birding stores sell a tarp that is designed to carpet the grass below your bird feeder. The grass is cut and the tarp is installed according to the manufacturer's directions. The design of the tarp features a loose weave that allows grass to grow up through it while trapping spent seeds and hulls that you would not want on your lawn. When the time comes to clean the bird feeder or take it down for the season (if you choose not to feed in summer), you simply unfasten the tarp and pull it up, enclosing all of the feeder waste within, while leaving an intact lawn behind.

5. Some bird—I think it might be a male red-wing blackbird—scolds and attacks me whenever I go out in my own backyard. This bird seems to be going berserk, for it dives at my head whenever I take three steps out into the yard. It really hurts when it hits me. I don't want to kill it, but I'm afraid that this crazy bird is going to cause me serious injury. How can I protect myself?

You have become an innocent victim of the territorial defense of a parent bird or a bird that has incorporated your backyard into its territory. The bird's goal is to drive off any would-be predators, and unfortunately, that includes you. Ornithologists refer to this behavior as "mobbing," which is most often observed when a noisy flock of smaller birds flies at a predator such as a hawk or a crow. One by one the smaller birds zoom toward the predator in a determined attempt to drive it out of their territory. Their distinctive and raucous calls alert others that a predator is in the area, at which point many other small birds may come to participate in the aerial mob.

Even though it sounds like a misnomer, mobbing can also be performed by a single bird whose philosophy seems to be that the best defense is a strong offense. Mockingbirds, blackbirds, and some species of flycatchers are often reported to mob inhabitants of houses and gardens, dive-bombing people and family pets alike. The bird seems to view the object of its attacks as a potential threat. When this type of combative behavior occurs, the best way to reclaim your backyard without having to resort to bloodshed is to use the bird's perceptions against it.

The bird will usually attack only the highest part of your body. (Notice that when you are standing, it

© Michael Francis/The Wildlife Collection

Here, a male red-winged blackbird is advertising his territory. Notice that this bird is showing both colors of his shoulder patches. A juvenile male or a male who is not reinforcing his claim to a territory with a display may hold his feathers so that only a thin yellow line is visible. Displaying males typically puff up their epaulets, making them larger and redder.

© Arthur Morris

This mockingbird seems alert but sedate as it perches in the sunlight of an Indian summer morning, but appearances can be deceptive. Although most territorial birds gradually stop their displays when the breeding season is over, mockingbirds defend both their summer nesting territory and their winter feeding territory. If you have mockingbirds in your backyard, listen for the grating, screeching call note that accompanies a territorial dispute. There's a good chance that the mockingbird is warning you away from "its" yard.

never flies at your torso or feet, but rather grazes the top of your head. If you bend over from the waist, it will attack the highest portion of your back.) To keep the bird farther away from your face, tuck a tall feather into your hatband or sweatband. The bird should then direct its attacks at this new higher point. If you don't want to wear something on your head, hold up one hand and the bird will fly at it. Small children should be taught this strategy, and infants and toddlers should be supervised when left in a backyard that contains a guarding bird.

6. There is a sick-looking bird on the ground below my feeder. Its feathers are all puffy and its eyes are closed. It doesn't move much, but rather shifts its weight from foot to foot every once in a while. How can I help?

Birds are such lively creatures that it is difficult to believe they, too, have their illnesses, some of which are fatal. Unless you are a trained veterinarian, there is little you can do for a sick bird beyond keeping it warm and protected from predators. Perhaps the best course of action is to do nothing. The bird will either get well on its own, or it will die and be eaten by a predator. If this is a migratory bird, it is against the law to handle it, and in many states federal permits are needed to legally possess a migratory bird. If the bird dies on your premises, wrap it up in a newspaper and dispose of it with your garbage. Be sure to wash your hands after handling any dead bird. If the carcass is in good condition, you may want to call the local natural history museum or nature center, as they may be interested in making a specimen of the bird. In the event that they do want the specimen, put the dead

This injured acorn woodpecker displays all the symptoms of a sick bird: It looks immobile and holds one wing in an awkward position, as though it were broken. Its feathers are all puffed up and its eyes are closed. Sadly, other than keeping an injured bird warm and sheltered from predators, there is little that the average person can do to help. Bird rehabilitation centers, however, specialize in treating injured birds. Ask your local natural history museum or nature center if there is such an organization in your area.

bird in a plastic bag and store it in your freezer until you deliver it to them. Don't worry about the bird contaminating your frozen food. The plastic and below-freezing temperature will prevent this from happening.

Make sure that it isn't your feeder that has made this bird sick. Thoroughly scrub down your feeder and birdbath. Douse them with undiluted household bleach, rinse with water, and allow to dry for several hours in direct sunlight. When you refill your feeder and birdbath, you will have the satisfaction of knowing that your kindness will not accidentally kill any birds.

7. A bird has built a nest in my mailbox. What should I do?

If your mailbox doesn't close tightly and you don't get frequent deliveries, you may unwittingly be creating a nesting habitat for many species of birds. Keep in mind that a nest is not a permanent inconvenience, since most birds fledge their nestlings within two to three weeks. If at all possible, leave the nest undisturbed until the young have flown. Alert your mail carrier to the situation so that he or she does not accidentally disrupt the nest. In order to continue receiving your mail, attach a waterproof bag to the outside of your mailbox and consider putting up nest boxes with entrance holes of appropriate sizes for your mailbox tenants.

© Hugh P. Smith Jr.

Mail call! Baby western bluebirds respond to a disturbance that may signal the arrival of a parent with vigorous begging and calling.

©Hugh P. Smith Jr.

Mud nests like this, complete with baby barn swallows, are typically found in buildings that are not used frequently, such as equipment sheds, barns, and garages that are often left partially open. If you find yourself with a nestful of unexpected tenants such as these, try to minimize your use of the building and allow the parents to fledge their young. Watching the parents raise their young and seeing the swallows fly free will be the rewards of your patience.

Birds will often build nests in porch light fixtures as well. If this happens, don't turn on the porch light, because the heat from the bulb may kill the developing young. Allow the birds to fledge their young, then remove the nest. This will help to discourage further nesting in your light fixture.

CHAPTER NINE

Diversions for the Bird-Fostering Elite

Does the following describe your situation? Feeding wild birds has become your passion. Your garden is a year-round haven for wild creatures. As the seasons flow on and the years tick by, birds come and go, and your yearly lists burgeon. You get a reputation around town as being an expert on the subject of fostering wild birds, but after a while, it begins to pall as you get a little bored with the beginner's feeding and fostering strategies that I've described up until now. This may be just the time to spice up your hobby by trying something different, something new, something wilder and a bit more unusual.

© Richard Day

Here, a suet log is filled and ready for customers.

THREE NATURAL FEEDERS

In winter, try to bring the birds right to your kitchen windowsill (or wherever you spend time looking out) by attaching a slab of wood with the bark left on. Let it be a little shorter than the sill so that the rough feeder can expand in wet weather. Secure the wood to the sill with finishing nails well sunk into the bark so that the birds won't hurt themselves as they peck at the bark. Scatter seed on this slab feeder, and when winter winds blow, birdseed will roll into the crevices of the bark, keeping it on the slab, ready for the kitchen-window birds. You should also melt some suet or warm some peanut butter gorp and press it into the crevices of the bark for little birds to glean.

If you have well-grown evergreens, consider converting one into a chest-high winter cave that will provide shelter for all your feathered clients. On the most sheltered side of the tree, trim branches back to the trunk to make a cave about two feet (61cm) square. Weave copper wire back and forth to create a platform across the lower branches of the cave. The wire will support a piece of turf that you will cut from the soil. Make sure that the turf has plenty of deep grass and soil attached. All kinds of ground-feeding, litter-scratching birds will appreciate this winter cave, because it gets them into shelter up and off the frozen snow- and ice-covered ground.

Scour the woods for an attractive feeder-log to hang where it is convenient for watching. Features to look for are natural cavities, such as walnut-size woodpecker holes, and gnarled branches studded with clinging, dry cones. The more woodpecker holes, small crevices, and cones, the better, because these will be receptacles for the melted suet that you will pour into cavities and dribble onto cones. In cold weather, the suet will harden and the small-size cavities will naturally exclude jays and invite little birds. You will have created a unique and natural chickadee, nuthatch, and titmouse feeder.

© Tom J. Ulrich

A skinned deer skull mounted on a tree offers lots of suet and bits of meat for small birds to feast on during the winter months. Freezing temperatures are necessary, however, to ensure the success of this bird-feeding method.

SKULLS IN THE TREES

This idea may seem extreme, but it makes perfect biological sense. I first encountered this unique bird-feeding method at an uncle's house, where I was startled to see three cow heads (one with long horns still attached) hanging fifteen feet (4.5m) in the air against a backdrop of pine needles. My uncle's log home had a deck along the second story, and the hanging skulls were the focal point of a high-in-the-trees bird-feeding area that I have never seen replicated anywhere.

There are, however, some caveats. This idea will work only if you have hard, cold winters, if your yard is secluded (so that the neighbors don't think you've gone mad; my Uncle Tommy lived in a rural farming community and his neighbors were a half mile [0.8km] away), and if you are not squeamish.

Most butchers will know how you can obtain a cow skull or other large skeletal elements with meat, gristle, and fat still attached, but hide removed. You will need to suspend these in high tree branches, perhaps fifteen feet (4.5m) off the ground, so that raccoons, foxes, dogs, and cats can't carry them off. Skulls are easiest to suspend because they have many natural holes and perforations for nerves and muscles that will be large enough to admit a quarter-inch (64mm) rope. A long, strong rope threaded through the rings of bone around the eyes of the cow and tied with nonslip knots will secure the skull. You can cleat the rope to the trunk of a tree to enable you to lower and remove the bones when the weather warms up. But all winter long, the skull will attract crowds of large and small hungry birds, and if you're a lazy bird feeder, you won't have to keep venturing outside to refill your suet containers as the snowdrifts deepen and the winter grinds on.

SUET TIPS FOR FEATHERED ACROBATS

If you want to encourage chickadees, redpolls, and siskins, take a pan of melted suet to a spruce, fir, or pine tree, and dip the tips of the needles into the warm liquid. The suet will harden, and once the small suet-loving birds realize that this resource is available, they will cling to the needles, delighting you with their seemingly effortless, upside-down gymnastics.

THE FEATHER GAME

In the spring, when swallows are building nests and flying about and hunting for nesting materials, try offering them feathers. This is especially fun for children. The idea is to find a hill that swallows swoop across. When you see a swallow coming, toss up a feather. With luck, the bird will pick it out of the air! Your luck will be best on a breezy day. A variation of this is to try to get the swallow to take the feather from your hand. Place a large feather between your thumb and index finger and hold your hand straight up over your head. Stand still in an open, breezy place, and chances are the swallow will take the feather. The birds prefer white, soft feathers but will take any color if they can't get white ones. This game is fun and is quite a reward for collecting feathers all year long.

© Tom J. Ulrich

Practicing for the feather game. Keep in mind, however, that this game will only work if you're on a hill frequented by swallows on a windy day.

This basket with nesting material is attached to a backyard feeder.

OFFER NESTING MATERIAL

Save any kind of string or thread *except* sewing thread or monofilament. These should be avoided because birds can become fatally entangled in them. For the same reason, never offer any pieces of thread or twine that are longer than four inches. You can buy commercially available nesting material or, for a fraction of the cost, save bakery string. You can also use string unraveled from burlap bags. Wash the burlap bag in cold water to make the material easier to handle, and then cut the cloth into four-inch squares. Unravel these and tie the burlap threads into bundles, which can be tied to shrubs or trees. Put out a dozen or so of these bundles in places where you can observe the birds' reactions, but be ready with replacements. The birds may keep you busy replacing the string as fast as they use it.

You can track the birds as they fly off with nesting material and spy on their nesting activities. This is one sure way to find those well-hidden nests. Watch a bird fly off with nesting material. You will probably lose sight of it, but don't give up. Walk to where you last saw the bird; stand quietly and watch. The builder will soon fly by with more material, and in this way, if you are patient, you will be able to discover where the nest is hidden.

As an alternative way to offer nesting material, try stuffing it into an onion bag and hanging it on your feeder.

HAND TAMING: THE ULTIMATE BIRD-FEEDING SPORT

If you have lots of time and lots of patience, try to get birds to feed from your hand. Sound incredible? Well, it's difficult, but not impossible. The easiest species to hand-tame are redpolls (60 percent are said to come to the hand), chickadees (50 percent), and purple finches (30 percent). If you are ever in the section of New York's Central Park called the Ramble and hear the squeaking calls of titmice, hold out your open hand (preferably with some food in it), stand still, and get ready for a tamed bird to sit on your shoulder or land on your hand. These birds have been tamed by many New York bird lovers who hand-feed them. Once you've fed a wild bird from your open hand, you'll be hooked.

Here is the method to try for hand-taming chickadees and other members of the tit family (*Parulidae*).

1. When your feeders are established and birds are regularly coming for a week or two, take all the seed and suet away.
2. One hour later, place a few sunflower seeds on some surface in the feeder area (a bird table or platform feeder works best here) where you can comfortably rest your arm and hand. Go inside or take a seat a distance away from the feeding area and listen for chickadees. When you hear them, go out to the feeder and get as comfortable as you can with your hand in position near the sunflower seeds on the feeder platform.
3. Be patient. Wait for the bird to come in. Do not move your hand. Keep still. If you get tired or impatient, leave the feeder area and rest inside the house.

Lots of patience will entice your feeder regulars to feed from your hand.

© Kent and Donna Dannen

Many species of birds can be tamed. Here, a Clark's nutcracker is being hand-fed.

4. Eventually the bird will come to the feeder with your hand on it. Stay still and listen to the bird's chatter. It may sound angry or nervous. Do not move. Allow the bird to take the few seeds from the platform.

5. When the farthest seeds have been taken, slowly move the remaining seeds closer to your hand. Your goal for the first day should be to have the bird feeding one foot (30.4cm) from your hand.

6. The second day, put the few seeds at the place where the bird came closest the day before. Put some seeds in your palm and settle back to wait. When the bird comes, begin talking softly to it, but don't look at it directly. Steal glances out of the corner of your eye. Don't lick your lips or swallow because the bird may be frightened by these "predatory actions."

7. Soon the bird will have taken the few seeds that were on the feeder, and the only ones remaining will be those in your hand. Continue your gentle conversation with the bird. Do not lick your lips or swallow and soon the bird will take the seed from your palm.

8. The bird will be nervous and skittish and will leap up when its toes first touch your skin. No doubt it is a strange, soft texture for bird feet. If the bird flies away, keep talking softly and don't move; if it is hungry, the bird will be back and will settle more comfortably on your hand.

9. Repeat this process a dozen times and when the bird shows no fear, you may begin to move your hand away from the feeder. It's important not to do this before your bird is ready. Watch the bird's actions and pay special attention to its abdomen. If you see it pulsate, you are frightening the bird. At the instant you see a pulse in the bird's stomach, you must freeze or your bird may spook and never return.

10. In time you will be able to make small movements and the bird will not be frightened. Eventually you may even be able to walk around with the bird on your hand. Most wonderful of all, there will come a time when the bird will fly to you, greet you, and expect and demand to be fed when you appear. Anyone who has had a tamed bird fly to them in greeting will know this to be a truly amazing sensation that is well worth all your patient training.

PROJECT FEEDERWATCH

Are songbird populations increasing or decreasing? Long-time bird feeders notice fluctuations in bird numbers and in volume of birdseed from season to season. Some years, the pine siskins and purple finches are literally dropping from the trees, while in other seasons, few are seen. In the United States and Canada, Project FeederWatch aims to document population changes. For five bird-feeding seasons, Project FeederWatch participants have recorded numbers of species feeding at backyard feeders. Data are analyzed by Cornell University's Lab of Ornithology or at Long Point Bird Observatory in Port Rowan, Ontario.

To join Project FeederWatch in the United States, write to Project FeederWatch, Cornell Laboratory of Ornithology, 159 Sapsucker Woods Road, Ithaca, NY 14850. To join Project FeederWatch in Canada, write to Project FeederWatch, Long Point Bird Observatory, P.O. Box 160, Port Rowan, Ontario N0E 1M0. (Please indicate if you wish to receive materials in French.)

CHAPTER TEN

Houses for the Birds

Does the following sound familiar? Brimming with enthusiasm and general goodwill, you put up a birdhouse in your backyard. As you hang it up, you imagine the prospective tenants who will soon investigate the premises and bring nesting materials. You can almost hear the songs that will defend this patch of territory. Before long there will be eggs inside, followed by the sounds of hungry young birds, and then one day "your" fledglings will emerge. You'll spy on them from a safe distance, admiring their growth and behavior. You are certain that one day you will have the satisfaction of having done something especially good for future generations of birds—giving them a safe place to raise their young.

Unfortunately, real events don't match your daydream. Months go by and your birdhouse is ignored. No birds even seem curious, and when you take down the birdhouse for the winter you find a nest of wasps inside. What went wrong?

Probably many things.

Birds have remarkably narrow tolerances for the range of situations in which they will build their nests, so they tend to be highly choosy. Each species has specific requirements for the size of the nest box entrance, as well as for the dimensions of the interior space. The nest box's distance from the ground; its exposure to sunlight, prevailing winds, and rainfall; and the quantity and quality of the surrounding vegetation all influence a bird's choice. Finally, the season during which you put out the nest box may also affect its acceptance by birds. Although this long list of influential factors may seem rather daunting, you will soon learn that it isn't difficult to get birds to nest in the houses you provide. All it takes is some planning, careful thought, and patience.

© John Glover

A birdhouse adds a charming focal point to this garden that features plenty of berries, flowers, and foliage to attract hummingbirds, insects, and insect-eating birds.

THE UNDERLYING CONCEPT OF BIRDHOUSES

So few of us have had contact with people who maintain nest boxes as a hobby that most of us do not understand the basic concept. When you erect a birdhouse, you are actually supplying the natural world with a cavity, a commodity that is rare in urban and suburban environments. Such a site can be enticing to cavity-nesting birds looking to set up housekeeping. A nest box basically mimics the holes that woodpeckers of various species and sizes excavate in dead trees to shelter their young.

Imagine the characteristics of a woodpecker nest and you are on your way to better understanding the functional qualities a birdhouse should possess. A woodpecker nest is dug in wood, a durable weatherproof material that breathes. The tree provides a solid foundation for landing and launching. There is only one opening that leads to the nest, which is an elongated, internal chamber. Gouged by the woodpecker who excavated it, the inside of this chamber is rough. The cavity is usually located in a dead tree, and often the entrance receives a large amount of sunlight and faces away from prevailing winds. Braided textures in the bark of the tree may channel rainwater around and away from the nest entrance. While there is usually a perch on a nearby branch where parents of young birds may sit, there is no perch at the entrance hole where a predatory squirrel, blue jay, starling, or sparrow hawk could lie in wait and gain easy access to the nestlings.

The concept of a birdhouse acting as a substitute woodpecker nest helps to provide an overall checklist of qualities to look for in a birdhouse that you either buy or build:

1.Wood. Your birdhouse should be made of wood. Until you are a birdhouse veteran, with several successfully fledged broods to your credit, stick to natural-looking, wooden birdhouses. Although a cute, cunningly painted troll cottage may tickle your aesthetic fancy, the birds may not approve. Ceramic birdhouses are another possibility, but they should be cautiously investigated, primarily to make sure that heat will not build up in them. Never use plastic in a birdhouse, because it traps heat that may kill your nesting birds.

If you are constructing a birdhouse yourself, any durable, non-splitting, weather-resistant wood that is easy to work with can be used. Cedar, redwood, and cypress are preferred over pine because they last longer and weather attractively; they also do not require paint. Spruce and the soft pines (white pine, sugar pine, and ponderosa) are also suitable, but they do not last as well without paint to protect them from the elements.

2. Entrance Holes. The entrance hole should be sized appropriately for the species of bird you wish to attract. Refer to "Birdhouse Dimensions" on page 116 for a list of the entrance hole measurements that are suited for specific cavity-nesting birds.You will notice that there is a considerable amount of overlap in these figures, so your birdhouse may not attract the exact species you intend.

3. Ventilation and Drainage Holes. Whether you make or buy a birdhouse, it will not be complete until it has several ventilation holes (three per side is a good number). These should be drilled above the level of the entrance hole so that they will allow hot air to escape. Drainage holes in the floor of the nest box are also important. These promote air circulation in hot weather and allow the nest to stay dry when rainwater enters. It is preferable to have four drainage

© Robert C. Simpson/Tom Stack & Associates

The size of an entrance hole is critically important. A bird's body should completely fill the entrance hole; there should be no extra room that would allow brood parasites or predators easy access.

holes, one for each side or corner. If you purchase a ready-made birdhouse that does not have ventilation and drainage holes, you should drill them in before offering the house to the birds.

4. Finish. The outside of your birdhouse may be painted with water-based enamel or exterior wood stain to prevent deterioration, but wood preservatives and sealers must be avoided because they give off lethal vapors. Never paint the inside of a birdhouse or use wood that feels sticky or smells of creosote.

5. Glue. You need a waterproof, weatherproof glue that will not stain wood.

6. Nails and Screws. Non-rusting nails will give your finished birdhouse a more attractive look. Any hardware that will be visible should be brass or brass-plated.

START IN THE RIGHT SEASON

Finding a spot for your birdhouse that will both please your target species and allow you to observe it easily is probably the most difficult task you face. Birdhouses should be in place by late February or early March, but at this time of year, before the trees have fully leafed out, it is difficult to find a suitable site. Because most cavity-nesting birds prefer their houses to have high exposure to sunlight, and hence avoid birdhouses that are in shady spots, the best strategy is to begin scouting locations in early autumn when the trees still have their leaves. If you have several houses ready, you may want to experiment by placing one in partial shade and one in full sunlight to let the birds tell you which sort of locality they prefer. Remember to allow for the territoriality of nesting birds and leave as much space as possible between nest boxes.

HOW MANY HOUSES?

A one-acre (0.4ha) property can probably support four small birdhouses and perhaps one larger one. Few birds tolerate close-nesting neighbors, so space out your birdhouses as much as possible. You can set up houses to attract a variety of species to your backyard, or you can concentrate on a single species. If you opt for the former, one type of bird you might like to entice is the wren. Wrens are such vivacious creatures that many people want a nesting pair more than any other kind of bird. Try putting up several wren houses in different locations. A house mounted on a pole in your vegetable garden may entice a male wren to build one of several "trial" nests for a female. If you would like the boxes in your backyard to focus on a single species, you might set up a string of bluebird or tree swallow boxes. Bluebird boxes should be placed about three hundred feet (91.4m) from one another, and tree swallow boxes should be a little over two hundred feet (60.9m) apart.

EXPOSURE

Before attaching it to a tree, consider how your birdhouse will perform in early spring cold spells as well as in summer's heat. In summer, the upper ventilation holes and lower draining holes will mitigate the inside temperature somewhat, but the direction in which the entrance hole faces will have a greater effect. Theoretically, to preserve heat in cold months, you should situate the nest box so that its

It's beautiful, but it's not for the birds! Look at the list of birdhouse dimensions (page 116) and you'll see that this foot-square house is much too large for any of the species that can fit in its 1½" entrance.

opening is facing away from the prevailing winds. Alternatively, if you are in an area that has very hot summers, it may be best to face the nest entrance toward the prevailing winds. Positioning a birdhouse successfully is a tricky maneuver that usually entails some degree of trial and error.

SECURITY

Your nest box must be solidly fixed to its tree so that a parent bird will not dislodge or jiggle it during takeoffs and landings. The only birds reported to nest in houses that sway are house wrens, though the inhabited wren houses that I've seen have all been firmly fixed. I therefore suggest that you nail yours securely in place.

The next element to consider in the safety department is security against predators. Nesting birds are preyed upon by cats, raccoons, squirrels, blue jays, starlings, kestrels, sharp-shinned hawks, tree-climbing snakes, and others. The less accessible your nest box is to these threatening creatures, the better. It is for this reason that none of the birdhouse plans in this chapter includes a perch. Although it seems instinctive to human designers to add a perch at a birdhouse's entrance hole, such an addition is actually detrimental, for it gives predators a convenient place to lurk. Perches are superfluous anyway, since cavity-nesting birds have no trouble alighting at the entrance of their nests. If you buy a birdhouse with a perch at the entrance, remove this unnecessary and harmful appendage immediately.

As soon as your birdhouse is set up and occupied, keep alert for predators and frighten away any that approach. You should further protect the entrance to the nest by attaching a predator guard that surrounds the entrance hole. This is a three-quarter- to one-inch-thick piece of wood with an entrance hole cut into its center. When it is nailed in place, the predator guard moves the contents of the nest farther out of the predator's reach.

Squirrels may try to enlarge the nest entrance by gnawing at it, so make a habit of inspecting your nest boxes daily and be prepared to add a second predator guard if the foes are persistent. To protect the nest against tree-climbing snakes, wind plastic deer mesh around the tree trunk; this will effectively snare and trap hunting snakes. If cats are a problem, consider encircling the tree trunk or pole that supports the birdhouse with a piece of aluminum flashing that is too wide for cats to span.

HOW HIGH?

Different species of birds have specific requirements about the height that is suitable for their nests. About five feet above the ground is appropriate for the houses of a wide range of cavity-nesters, including bluebirds, chickadees, titmouses, flycatchers, nuthatches, prothonotary warblers, tree swallows, downy woodpeckers, and wrens. If you are a beginner, start by setting up your birdhouses at your eye level. Since you'll be checking them on a regular basis, you might as well make the process as easy as possible for yourself. One of the problems with putting up birdhouses is that it's almost impossible to predict which species will adopt your nest box as a home. If a house is ignored, try moving it a bit higher.

THE LANDLORD'S ROUTINE

It is not enough to put up nest boxes that are safe and secure; you must monitor them from time to time, ensuring that the species you wish to favor are nesting and checking to eject squatters. Aggressive, non-native species such as house finches, starlings, and house sparrows deprive native birds of their normal nesting places, so you'll probably want to evict these invasive birds. Meadow mice and other rodents are also creatures that you may choose to evict if they take up residence in your nest box. However, if a native species of bird begins to build in a nest box you intended for a different species, rather than ejecting these tenants, consider erecting an additional box for the bird you wish to attract.

The following equipment will be handy as you inspect your nest boxes: jackknife, screwdriver, pyrethrum-based insecticide, bar of soap, and a long-handled brush. Before opening a nest box, watch for a few minutes to see if insects are flying in and out. If wasps have taken over, you may want to quickly spray the box and retreat to safety. An even better plan is to wait to spray the box at sunset when all of the

If you decide to copy the design of this charming martin house, remove the perches. Since martins need a significant amount of space to glide before landing, birdhouses are most appealing to them when placed in the midst of an open field or near a stretch of open water.

inhabitants are at home. The next day, remove the wasps' comb and rub the inside of the box with bar soap to discourage a second infestation.

If there aren't any insects flying in and out, birds may have begun to build. Tap on the nest box. Often baby birds will begin to screech a response. If the box has an active nest, you may safely open the top and peek inside. Don't stay too long, however, because your presence may attract predators or frighten the parents and cause them to desert the nest.

Return to the nest box when the young have fledged. Tap on the outside again and if there is no noise from within, open it up. If the nest is empty, use a long-handled brush to remove the old nest. This will encourage the tenants to begin a new brood. Inspect the bottom of the box for crawling insects and mites, and scrub out the corners.

Once the nesting season is over, remove old nests again. Birdhouses that are nailed in place may either be taken down for the winter or left as winter housing for wildlife. Begin this maintenance routine once again in the early spring by cleaning out any debris that accumulated over the winter.

HOUSING PLANS

Consider the birdhouse plans on the following pages as a kind of wish list. Not everyone has the space and habitat needed to accommodate the variety of unusual birds represented here, such as ospreys and purple martins, but many people can accommodate house wrens and chickadees. The basic birdhouse plan (see page 117) can be varied to embrace different species by changing the dimensions of the house as well as the size of the entrance hole (see the chart below).

BIRDHOUSE DIMENSIONS

Birds	*Floor*	*Roof*	*Sides & Back**	*Diameter of Entrance Hole*
Bluebird, Eastern, Mountain, & Western	5 x 5	5 x 6	5 x 8–12	1⅜ to 1½
Chickadee	4 x 4	4 x 6	4 x 8–10	1⅛
Great Crested Flycatcher	6 x 6	6 x 8	6 x 8–10	1¾ to 2
Nuthatch, Pygmy & Red-breasted	4 x 4	4 x 6	4 x 8–10	1¼
Nuthatch, White-breasted	4 x 4	4 x 6	4 x 8–10	1⅜
Titmouse	4 x 4	4 x 6	4 x 8–10	1¼ to 1⅜
Tree Swallow	5 x 5	5 x 7	5 x 6–8	1⅜ to 1½
Woodpecker, Downy	4 x 4	4 x 6	4 x 8–10	1¼
Woodpecker, Pileated	8 x 8	8 x 10	8 x 12–20	3 to 4
Woodpecker, Red-headed	6 x 6	6 x 8	6 x 12–15	2
Wren, Carolina	4 x 4	4 x 6	4 x 6–8	1½
Wren, House	4 x 4	4 x 6	4 x 6–8	1 to 1¼

*Cut the back two inches longer so that you will be able to hang the house on a tree.

(All measurements are in inches—for metric conversions, see page 117.)

BASIC BIRDHOUSE PLAN

Note: The dimensions given here are appropriate for bluebirds and tree swallows. This basic plan may be used in conjunction with the dimensions listed on page 116 to attract other species.

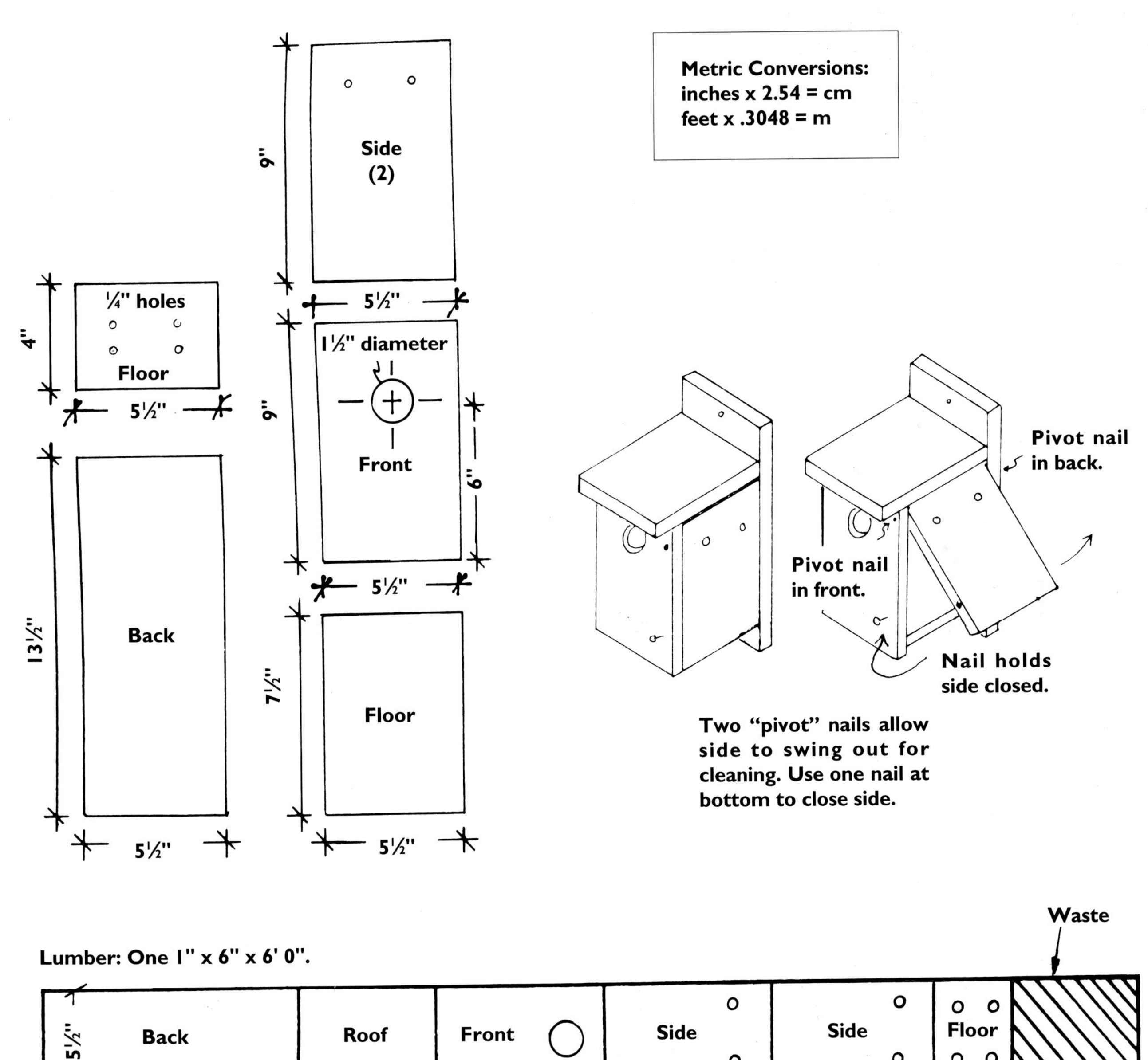

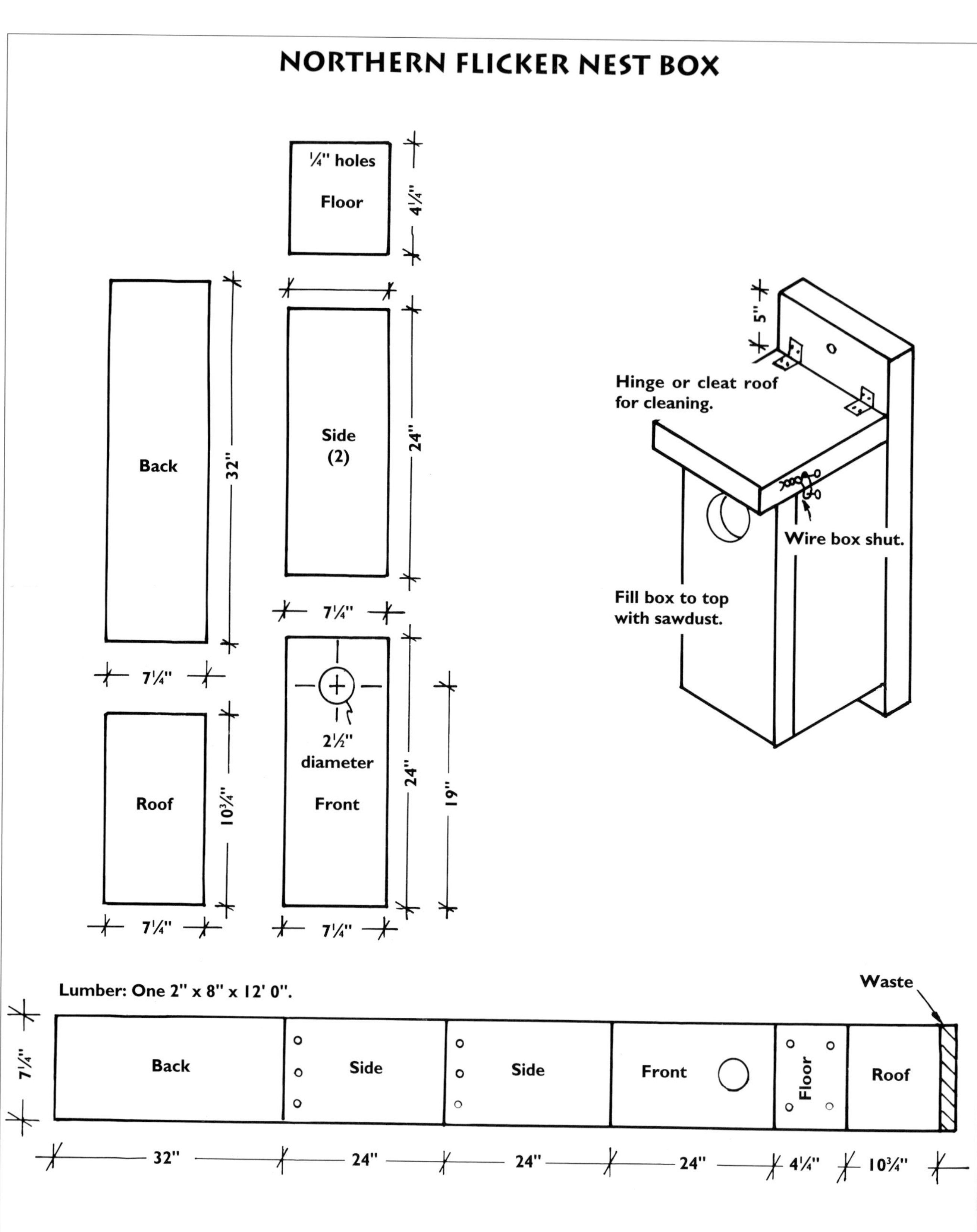
NORTHERN FLICKER NEST BOX
¼" holes
Floor
4¼"
Back
32"
7¼"
Side
(2)
24"
7¼"
Roof
10¾"
7¼"
2½"
diameter
Front
24"
19"
7¼"
5"
Hinge or cleat roof
for cleaning.
Wire box shut.
Fill box to top
with sawdust.
Lumber: One 2" x 8" x 12' 0".
Waste
7¼"
Back
Side
Side
Front
Floor
Roof
32"
24"
24"
24"
4¼"
10¾"

AMERICAN ROBIN, BARN SWALLOW, AND EASTERN PHOEBE NEST SHELF

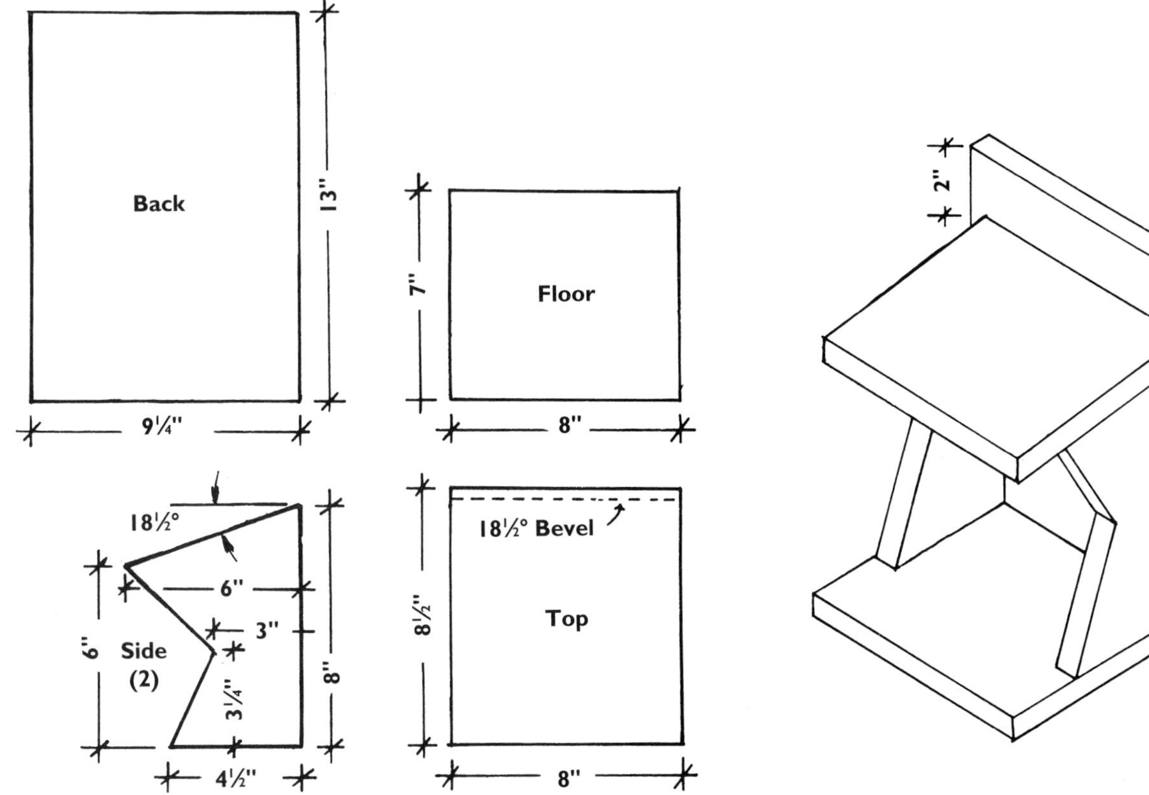

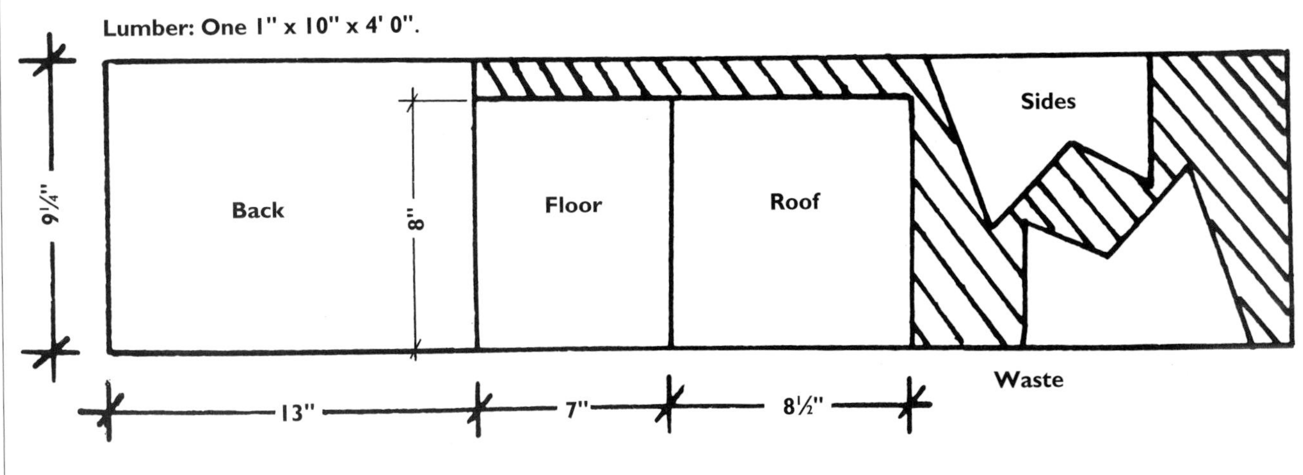

PURPLE MARTIN HOUSE

Materials:
4' x 8' x ¼" plywood.
2" x 2" x 6" for chimney.
1" x 2" x 14' for base.
1" x 1" x 8' for corner blocks.
4" x 8" metal window screen.
4" x 4" x 14' cedar post.

Place ½" dowel railing around balcony to keep young from falling.

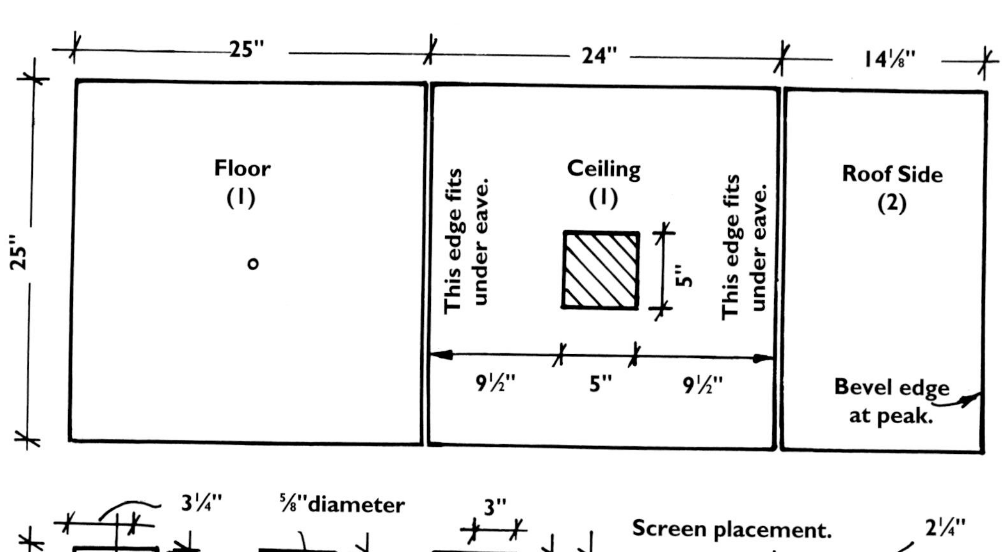

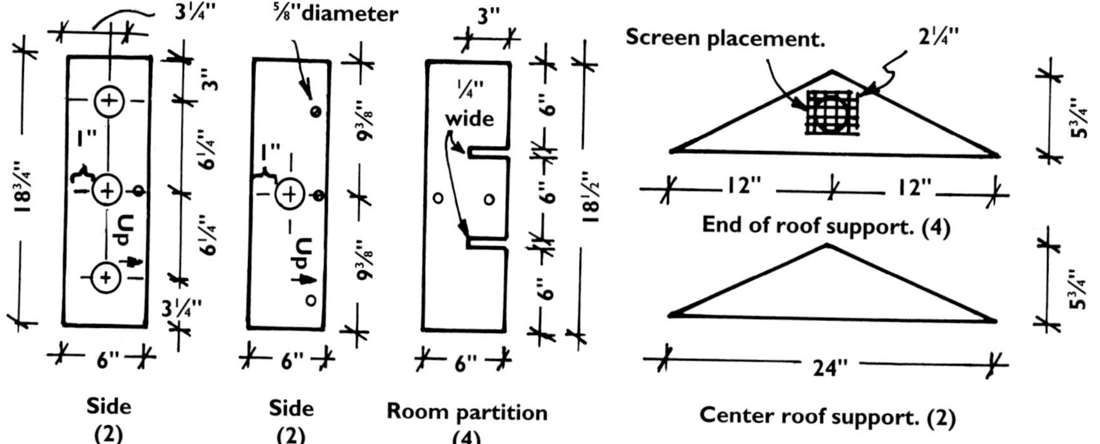

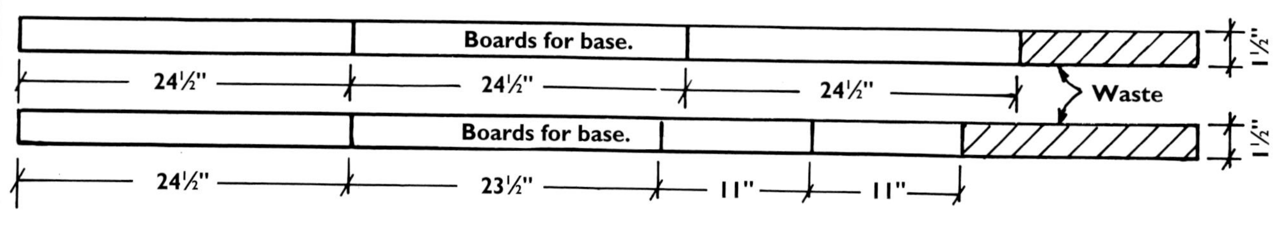

PURPLE MARTIN HOUSE
(CONTINUED)

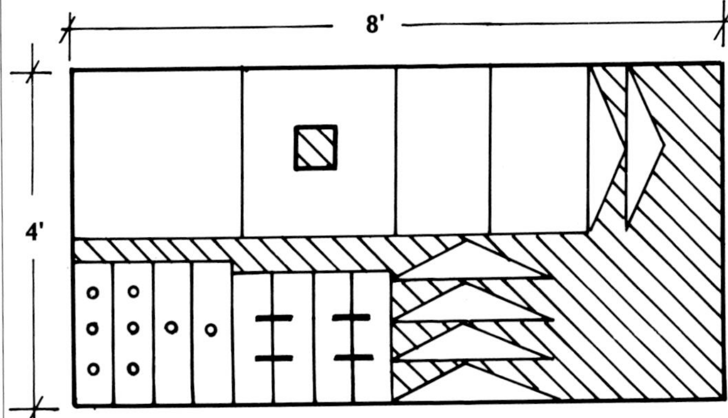

Layout pattern.

The pattern above shows how to cut out a martin house from one sheet of plywood.

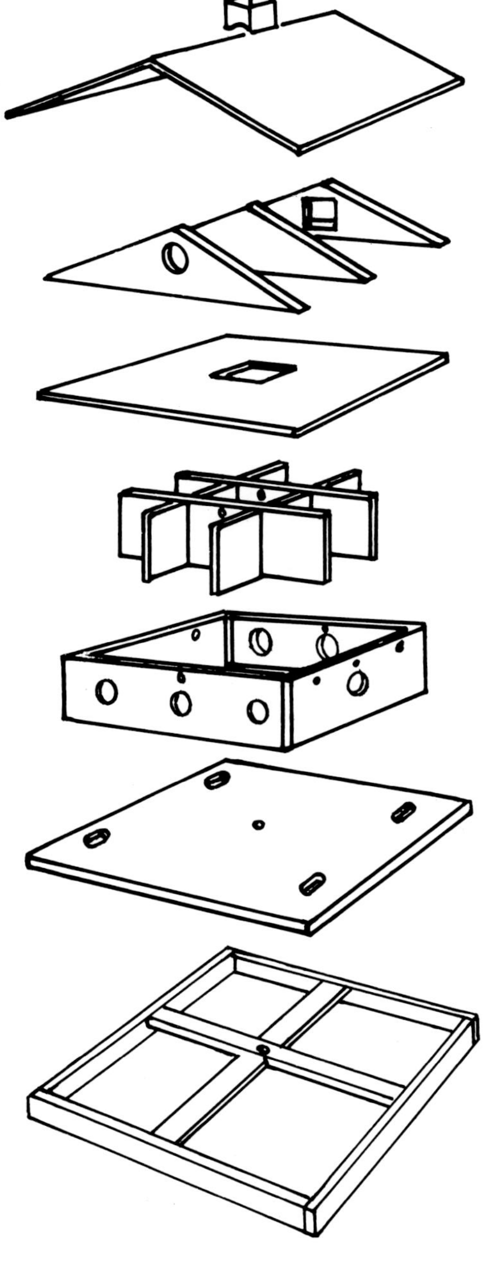

Expanded view of Martin House. A threaded rod inserts through the base and up through the chimney.

Entrance hole diameter: 2¼".

Locate ⅝" ventilation holes 1" below top edge of sides.

*For sides, measurement from floor to center of entrance holes = 2⅛".

Note: This plan is for a one-story house. To add a second story, make one more ceiling unit (25" x 25"), four more sides, and four more room partitions.

MOURNING DOVE NEST BASKET

Materials: One 12" x 12" piece of hardware cloth.

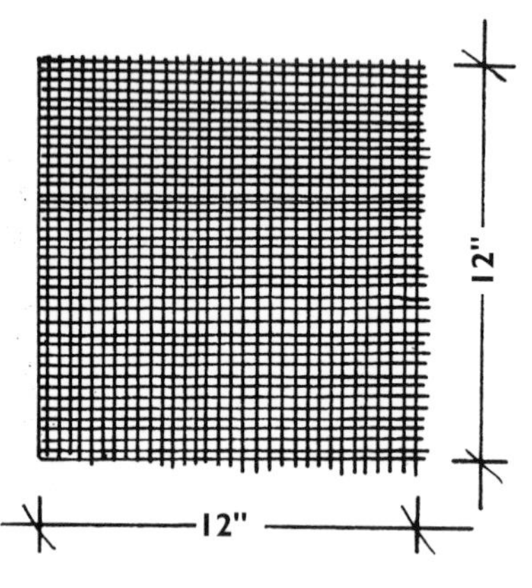

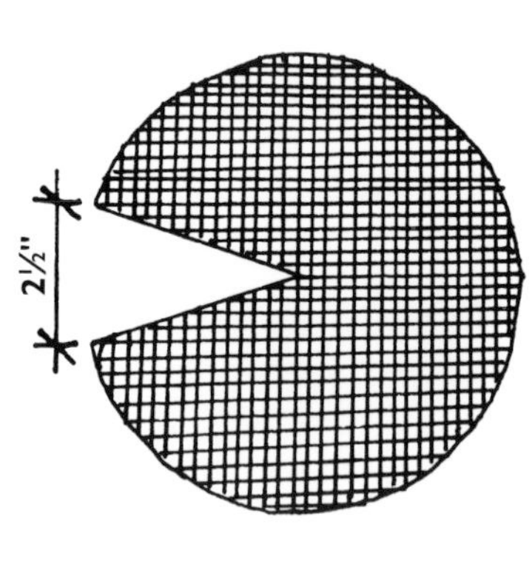

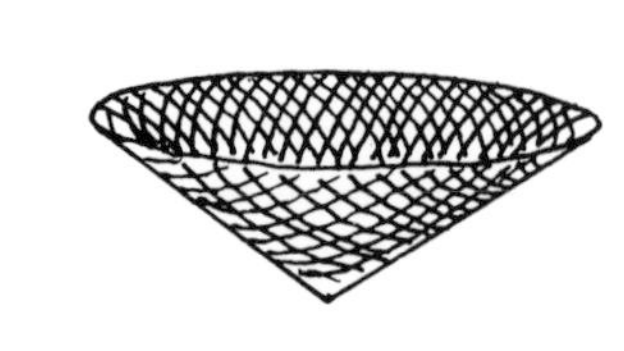

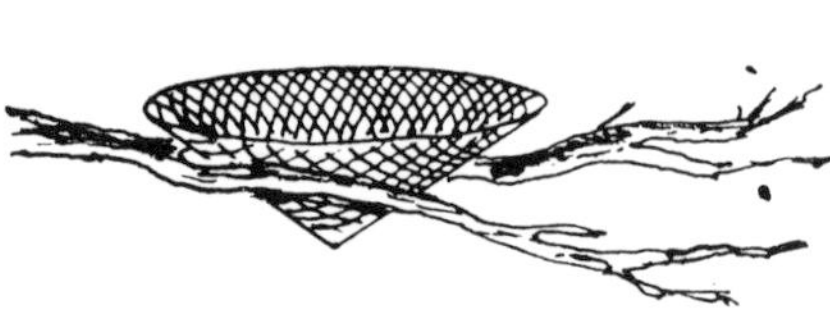

Cut with tin snips to form a circle. Cut out a narrow pie-shape, and wire edges together to form a cone. Wire and/or staple cone into the crotch of a tree limb.

GREAT BLUE HERON AND DOUBLE-CRESTED CORMORANT NEST PLATFORM

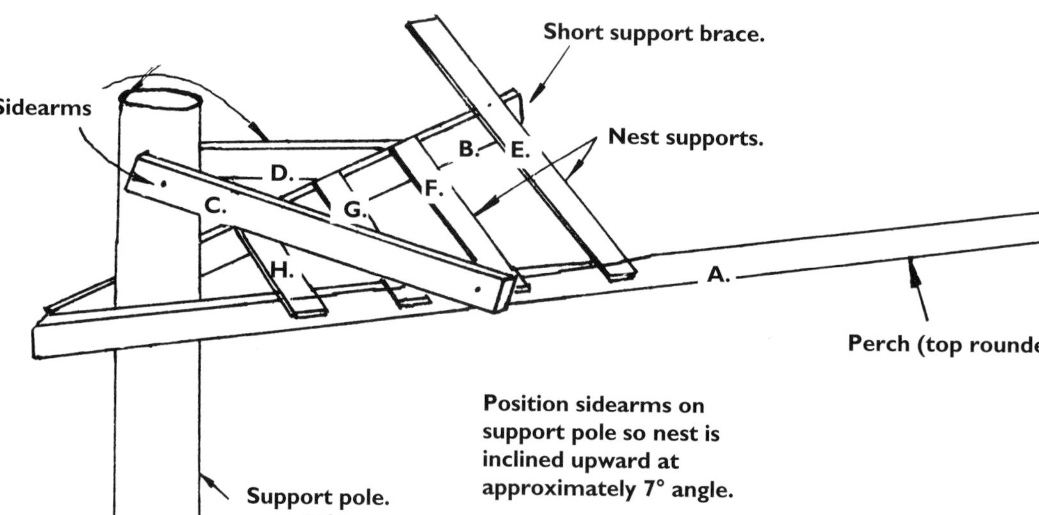

Position sidearms on support pole so nest is inclined upward at approximately 7° angle.

Wire armful of sticks onto lath nest supports to stimulate use.

Lumber:
A. 2" x 2" x 7'.
B. 2" x 2" x 30".
C. 1" x 2" x 26½".
D. 1" x 2" x 26½".
E. 1" x 2" x 39".
F. 1" x 2" x 19½".
G. 1" x 2" x 19¼".
H. 1" x 2" x 17⅞."
One 30' cedar support pole/three platforms.

MALLARD NEST BASKET

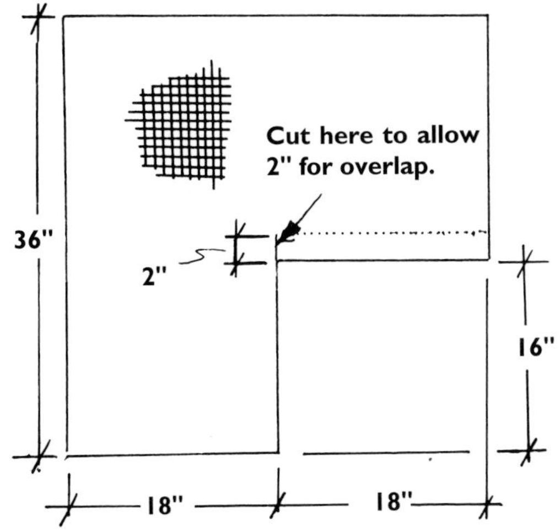

Basket pattern.

Materials:
8' support pipe, 1½" diameter.
2' 2" basket pipe, 1" diameter.
13' 6" steel rod, ¼" diameter.
3' x 3' hardware cloth, ½" mesh.

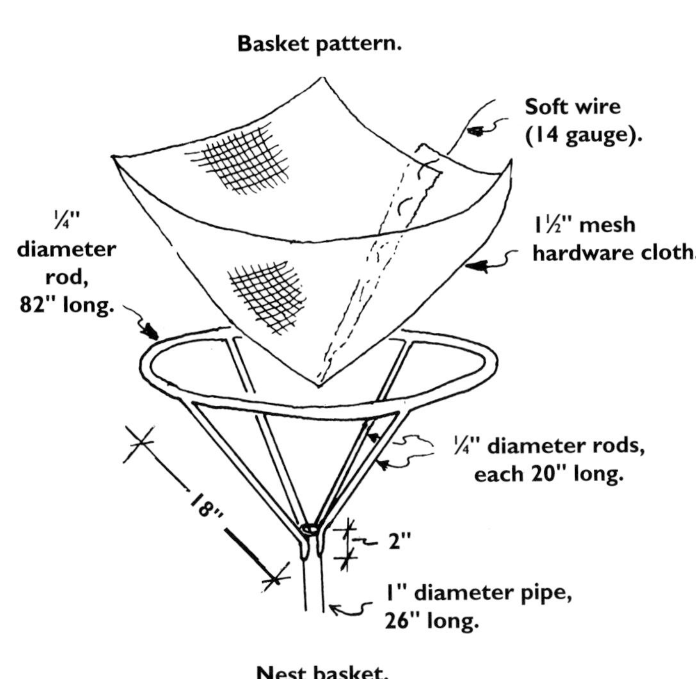

Nest basket.

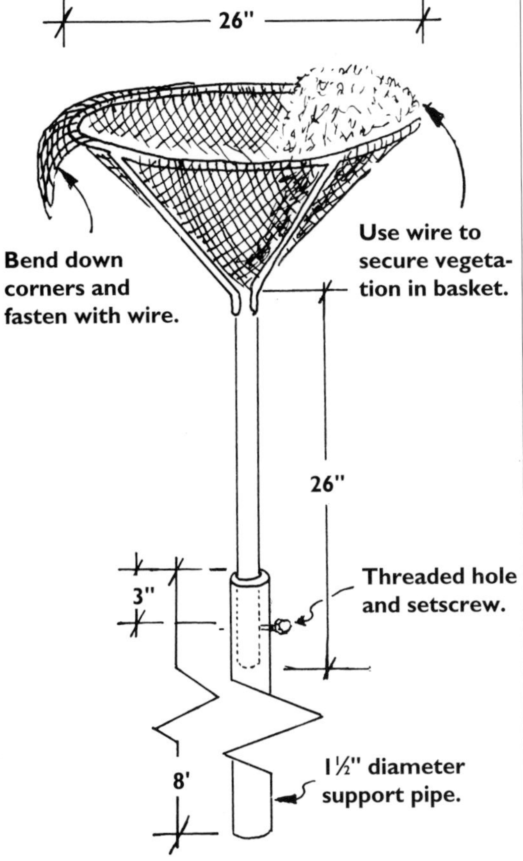

Frame and basket assembly.

OSPREY NEST PLATFORM

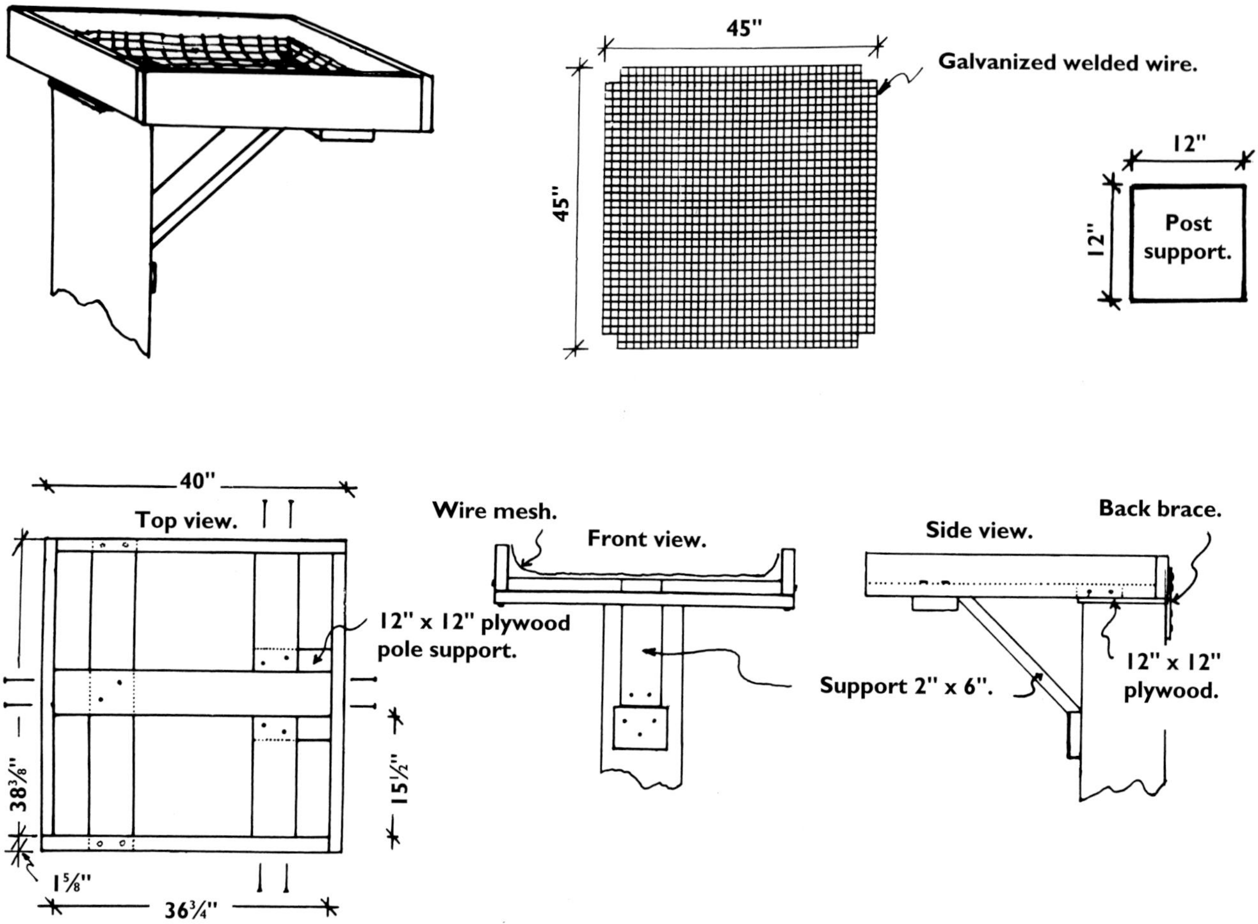

45"
Galvanized welded wire.
45"

12"
12"
Post support.

40"
Top view.
12" x 12" plywood pole support.
38⅜"
15½"
1⅝"
36¾"

Wire mesh.
Front view.
Support 2" x 6".

Side view.
Back brace.
12" x 12" plywood.

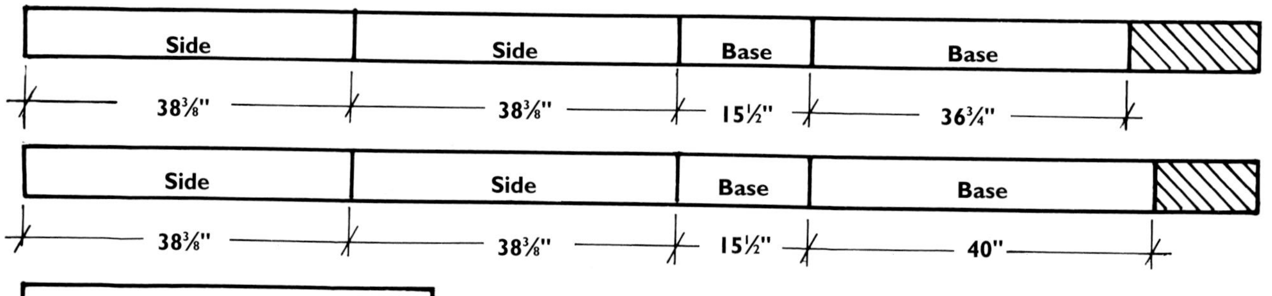

Side	Side	Base	Base
38⅜"	38⅜"	15½"	36¾"

Side	Side	Base	Base
38⅜"	38⅜"	15½"	40"

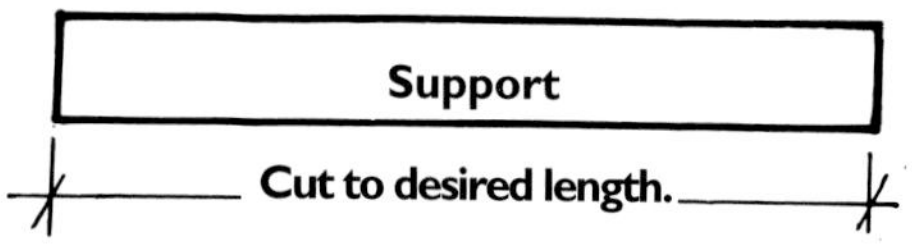

Support
Cut to desired length.

Lumber:
Two 2" x 6" x 12' cedar boards.
One 2" x 6" x 4' cedar board.
One 12" x 12" x ½" exterior plywood.
One 20' or 30' cedar support pole.

BARRED OWL NEST BOX

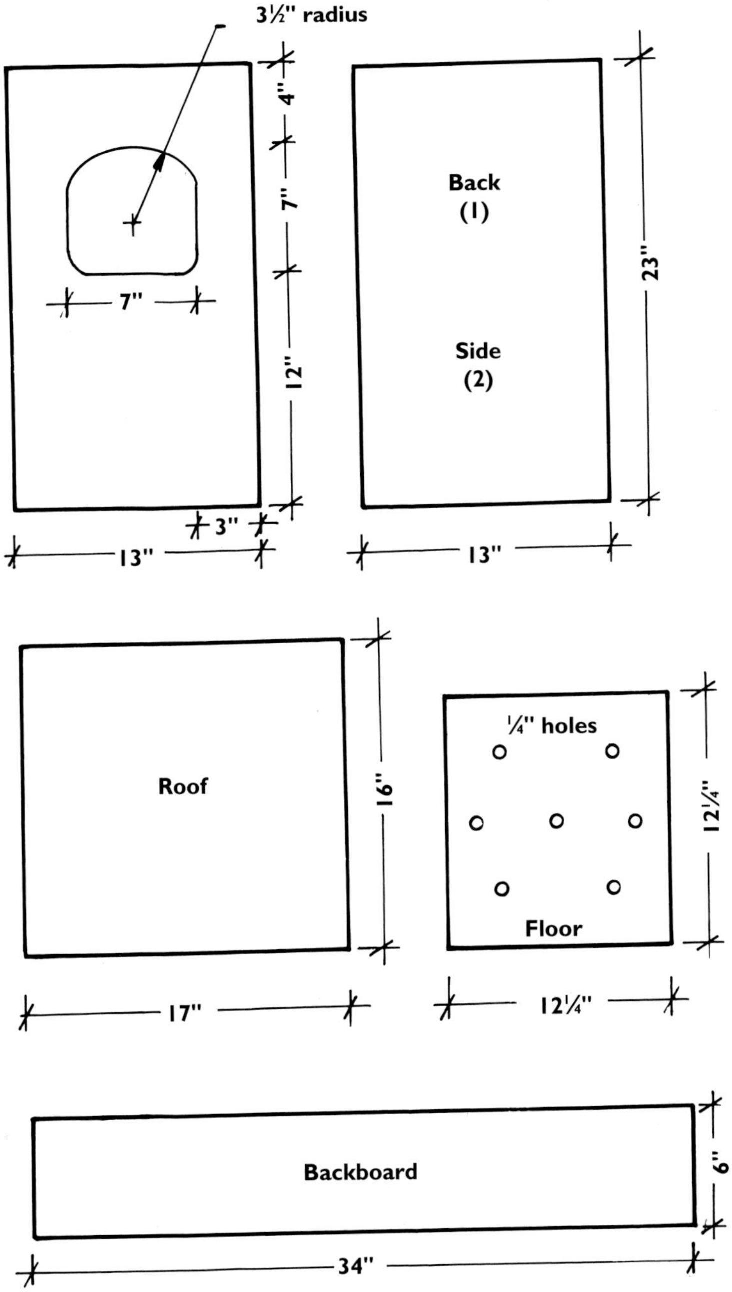

3½" radius
4"
7"
7"
12"
3"
13"
Back
(1)
Side
(2)
23"
13"
Roof
16"
17"
¼" holes
Floor
12¼"
12¼"
Backboard
6"
34"

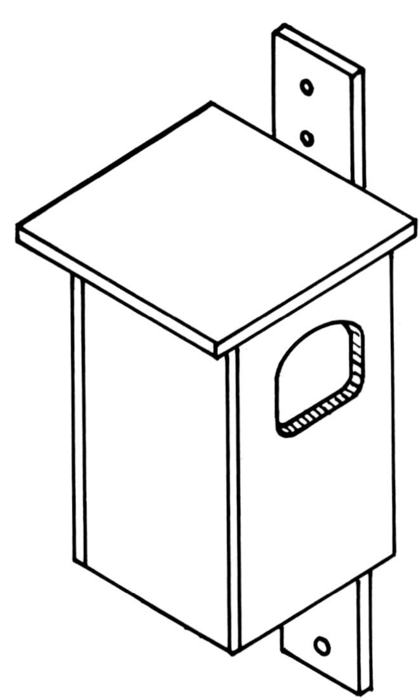

Note: No hinged door needed.
Clean through entrance hole.

Floor
Front
Back
Roof
16"
17"
Side
Side
Backboard
4'
4'

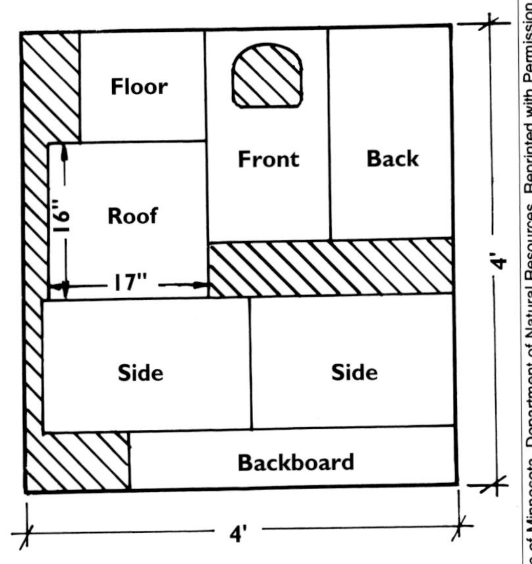

Lumber: One 4' x 4' x ¾" sheet exterior plywood.

INDEX